The Handy Concordance of the Quran

The Handy Concordance of the Quran

AURANG ZEB AZMI

Goodword

First published in 2002
Reprinted 2009
© Goodword Books 2009

Goodword Books
1, Nizamuddin West Market, New Delhi - 110 013
email: info@goodwordbooks.com
Printed in India

www.goodwordbooks.com

A

Aaron Harun هارون

    What they left behind 2:248
    His family 6:84
    Made deputy of Moses 7:142, 2:30, 25:35
    Sent to Pharaoh 10:75
    His sister 19:28
    His advice to his nation 20:90
    Given criterion 21:48
    About his eloquency 26:13, 28:34

Abase Ahana أهان

    Whom God abases, there is none to honour him (22:18)
    See also, 89:16

Abiding Baqi باقي See Enduring

Abode Bayt بيت See House

Abode Dar دار

    Take your joy in your habitation (11:65)
    The Last Abode is better for those that are god-fearing (6:32)
    Surely the Last Abode is life (29:64)
    See also, 2:84, 85, 94, 243, 246, 3:195, 4:66, 6:32, 127, 135, 7:78, 91, 145, 169, 8:47, 10:25, 11:67, 94, 12:109, 13:22, 24, 25, 31, 42, 14:28, 16:30, 17:5, 22:40, 28:37, 77, 81, 83, 29:37, 33:27, 29, 35:35, 38:46, 40:39, 52, 41:28, 59:2, 8, 9, 60:8,9

Abomination Rijs رجس

Wine and arrow-shuffling, idols and divining-arrow are an abomination (5:90)

God only desires to put away from you abomination (33:33)

See also 6:125,145, 7:71, 9:95, 125, 10:100, 22:30.

Abomination Fahisha فاحشة See Indecency

Abraham Ibrahim إبراهيم

Fulfilled God's Commands (2:124)
And Ka'ba 2:125-127, 3:96,97
Religion of 2:130,135
Not Jew or Christian 3:67
Not pagan 3:95
Rejects worship of heavenly bodies 6:75-79
Argues with sceptics 2:258
Argues with his father against idolatory 6:74,19:41-50
Argues with his people against idols 21:51-71,26:70-82, 29:16-18, 24-25, 37:83-98
On life to the dead 2:260
Preaches to his people 6:80-83
Prays for his father 9:113-114,26:86
Sacrifice of his son 37:99-111
Angels visit him to announce the birth of his son 11:69-73, 15:51-56,51:24-30
Pleads for Lut's people 11:74-76
His prayer 14:35-41,26:83-87
A model 16:120-123
Safe in the fire 21:69
Book of 53:37; 87:19
His example in dealing with Unbelievers 60:4-6

Abstinence Ta'affuf تعفف

Supposes them rich because of their abstinence (2:273)

Abu Lahab Abu Lahab (Uncle of the Prophet) أبو لهب
Perish the hands of Abu Lahab, and perish him (111:1)

Abundant-rain Midrar مدرار See Torrent

Accept as a true Saddaqa صدّق See Confirm

Acceptance Ridwan رضوان See Good pleasure

Account Hisab حساب See Reckoning

Accursed Rjim رجيم

And guarded them from every accursed Satan (15:17)
When thou recite the Qur'an, seek refuge in Good from the accursed Satan (16:98)
See also, 3:36, 15:17, 34,38: 77,81:25

Accusation of sinfulness Aththama أثم See Cause of sin

Accusation of sinfulness Tathim تأثيم See Cause of sin

Accuse Rama رمى See Throw

Act 'Amila عمل See Do

Act piously Ittaqa إتقى See Fear

Act unjustly Zalama ظلم See Wrong

Adam Adam آدم

Creation 2:30-34
Fall 2:35-39,7:19,26
Was chosen by Allah 3:33
Jesus is like him, 3:59
Two sons (Abel and Cain) 5:27-31
Iblis denied to bow down before him, 7:11, 17:61, 20:116
Was promised 20:115

Satan is their enemy, 20:117
Tempted by Satan 20:120-121

Adobe Umm أم See Mother

Adornment Zinah زينة

Take your adornment at every place of worship (7:31)
We have appointed all that is on the earth as an adornment for it (18:7)
We have adorned the lower heaven with the adornment of the planets (37:6)
See also, 7:32, 10:88,11:15,16:8, 18:28, 46, 20:59, 87, 24:31, 60, 28:60, 79, 33:28,37:6

Adversity Darra' ضرّاء See Hardship

Affection Mawaddah مودة See Love

All-subtle Latif لطيف

He is the all subtle, the all aware (6:103)
See also, 12:100, 22:63, 31:16, 33:34, 42:19, 67:14

All beings Alamin عالمين

Praise belongs to God, the Lord of all being (1:2)
God desires not any injustice to living beings (3:108)
We preferred them above all beings (45:16)
See also, 2:47, 122, 131, 251, 3:33, 42, 96, 97, 108, 5:20, 28, 115, 6:45, 71, 86, 90, 162, 7:54, 61, 80, 104, 121, 140, 10:10, 37,12:104, 15:70, 21:71, 91, 107, 25:1, 26:16, 23, 47, 77, 98,109, 127, 145, 164, 165, 180, 192, 27:8, 44, 28:30, 29:6, 10, 15, 28, 32:2, 37:79, 87, 182, 38:87, 39:75, 40:64, 65, 66, 41:9, 43:46, 44:32, 45:36, 56:80, 59:16, 68:52, 69:43,81:27,29,83:6

All-gentle Latif لطيف See All-subtle

All-knowing Alim عليم

God is all-embracing, all-knowing (2:115)
He has knowledge of everything (2:29)
See also 2:3,9, 95, 127, 137, 158, 181, 215, 224, 227, 231, 244, 246, 247, 256, 261,268, 273, 282, 283, 3:34, 35, 63, 73, 92, 115,119, 121, 154, 4:11, 12, 17, 24, 26, 32, 35, 39, 70, 104, 111, 127, 147, 148, 170, 176, 5:74, 76. 97, 6:13, 83, 96,101, 115, 128, 139, 7:109, 112, 200, 8:17, 42, 43, 53, 61, 71, 75, 9:15, 28, 44, 47, 60, 97, 98, 101, 106, 110, 115, 10:36, 65, 79, 11:15, 2:6, 19, 34, 50, 55, 76, 83, 100, 15:25, 53, 86, 16:28, 70, 21:4, 52, 59, 23:51, 24:18, 21, 28, 32, 35, 41, 58, 59, 60, 64, 26:34, 37, 220, 27:6, 78, 29:5, 60, 62, 30:54, 31:23, 34, 33:1, 40, 51,54, 4:26, 35:8, 28, 38, 44, 36:38, 79, 81, 39:7,40:2, 41:12, 36, 42:12, 24, 50, 43:9, 84, 44:6, 48:4, 26, 49:1, 8, 13, 16, 51:28, 30, 57:3, 6, 58:7, 60:10,62:7, 64:4, 11, 66:23,67:13,76:30

All-merciful Rahman رحمن

In the name of God, the merciful, the compassionate (1:1)
Thou seest not in the creation of the All-merciful any imperfection (67:3)
See also, 1:3, 2:163, 13:30, 17:110, 19:18, 26,44, 45, 58, 61,69,75,78,85,87,88,91,92,93,96,20:5,90,108,109, 21:26, 36, 42, 112, 25:26, 59, 60, 63, 26:5, 27:30, 36:11, 15, 23, 52, 41:2, 43:17, 19, 20, 33, 36, 45, 81, 50:33, 55:1, 59:22, 67:3, 19, 20, 29, 78:37, 38

All-preserving Muhaymin مهيمن See Assuring

Al-Lat Al-Lat اللات

Have you considered Al-Lat and Al-Uzza (53:19)

All-being Barr بَرّ See Pious

All-forgiving Ghaffar, Ghafur غفور ، غفار

    I am All-forgiving to him who repents (20:82)
    God is even All-forgiving (25:70)
    See also, 38:66,39:5,40:42,71:10
    For Ghafur, 2:173, 182, 192, 199, 218, 225, 226, 235,3:31,89, 129,155, 4:23, 25, 43, 96, 99, 100, 106, 110, 129, 152, 5:3, 34, 39, 74, 98, 10: 107, 11:41, 12:53, 98, 14:36, 15:49, 16:18, 110, 115, 119, 17:25, 44, 18:58, 22:60, 24:5, 22, 33, 62, 25:6, 70, 27:11, 28:16, 33:5, 24, 50, 59, 73, 34:2, 15, 35:28, 30, 34, 41, 39:53,41:32, 42:5, 23, 46:8, 48:14, 49:5, 14, 57:28, 58:2, 12, 60:7, 12, 64:14,66:1, 67:2, 73:20, 85:14

All-giver Wahhab وهاب

    Surely thou are the All-giver (38:35)
    See also 3:8,38:9

All-holy Quddus قدوس

    He is the king, the all-holy, the all-peaceable (59:23)
    See also 62:1

All-loving Wadud ودود

    Surely my Lord is All-compassionate, All-loving (11:90)
    See also, 85:14

Allow vt. Adhina أذن See Guide

All-pardoning Afuw عفوّ

    God is All-pardoning (4:43)
    See also, 4:99,149,22:60,58:2

All-provider Razzaq رزاق

    Surely god is the All-provider (51:58)

All-thankful Shakur شكور

Surely He is All-forgiving, All thankful (35:30)

In that are signs for every man enduring, thankful (42:33)

See also, 14:5, 17:3, 31:31, 34:3, 19, 35:34, 42:23, 64;17

Alms Sadaqah صدقة See Freewill offering

Alter Ghayyara غيّر See Change

Alteration Baddala بدّل See Substitute

Altered mud Hama' حما See Moulded mud

Altering Tahwil تحويل See Change

Al-Uzza Uzza عزى

Have you considered Al-Lat and Al-Uzza (53:19)

Amazing Fary فري See Monstrous

Ancient-Ones Awwalun أوّلون

These are nothing but the fairy-tales of the ancient-ones (6:25)

Did We not destroy the ancients (77:16)

See also, 8:31, 38, 9:100, 15:10, 13, 16:24, 17;59, 18:55, 21:5, 23:24, 68, 81, 83, 25:5, 26:26, 136, 184, 196, 27:168, 28:36, 35:43, 37:17, 126, 43:6, 8, 44:8, 46:17, 56:13, 39, 48, 49, 68:15, 77:38, 83:13

Anger Ghdab غضب

Exceed not therein, or My anger shall alight on you (20:81)

Those who avoid the heinous sins and indecencies and when they are angry forgive (42:37)

See also, 1:7, 2:61,90, 3:112, 4:93, 5:60, 7:71, 152, 154,8:16,16:106, '20:81, 24:9, 42:16, 37, 48:6, 58:14, 60:13

Anguish Ghamm غمّ See Grief

Animal Bahimah بهيمة See Beast

Animal Dabbah دابة See Beast

Any Ahad أحد See One

Apostasy Fitnah فتنة See Trial

Apostle Rasul رسول See Messenger

Apostle Hawariy حواري

> The Apostles said "we will be helpers of God" (3:52)
> See also, 5:111, 112, 61:14

Appoint Farda فرض

> We know what We have imposed upon them (33:50)
> God has ordained for you the absolution of your oath (66:2)
> See also 2:197,236,237,4:7,118,24:1,28:85,33:38

Argument Hujjah حجّة

> There is no argument between us and you (42:15)
> Their argument is null and void (42:16)

Ark Fulk فلك See Ship

Arm Adud عضد See Helper

Army Jund جند See Garment

Arrange Rattala رتل See Chant

Arrow-shuffling Maysir ميسر

> Arrow-shuffling, idols and divining arrows are an abomination (5:90)

See also 2:219,5:91

Ascribe Da'a دعا See Call

Ascribe vt Daa دعا See Call

Ask leave, Ista'dhana إستأذن

> The way is open only against those who ask leave of thee (9:93)
> Those who ask thy leave, those are they that believe in God (24:62)
> See also 9:44,45,83,86,24:59,62,33:13

Ask performing Ista'dhana إستأذن See Ask leave

Assault Batsh بطش

> Surely thy Lord's assault is terrible (85:12)
> We destroyed men stronger in valour than they (43:8)
> See also 50:36
> For verb, 7:195,26:130,28:19,44:16

Assemble Hashar حشر See Musbr

Assemble vt Hashara حشر See Muster

Assemblies Majalis مجلس

> Make room in the assemblies (58:11)

Associate Sharik شريك

> No associate has He (6:136)
> What is for God reaches their associates (6:136)
> See also, 4:12, 6:22, 94, 100, 136, 137, 139, 163, 7:190, 195, 10:28, 34, 35, 66, 71, 13:16, 33, 16:27, 86, 17:111, 18:152, 25:12, 28:62, 64, 74, 30:13, 28, 40, 34:27, 35:40, 39:29, 41:47, 42:21, 68:41

Associate vt Ashraka أشرك

If thou associate other gods with God, thy work shall surely fail (39:65)

Serve God and associate not any partners with Him (4:36)

See also 2:105, 135, 221, 3:64, 67, 95, 151, 186, 4:16, 36, 48, 116, 5:72, 82, 6:14, 19, 22, 23, 41, 64, 78, 79, 80, 81, 82, 88, 106, 107, 121, 137, 148, 151, 161, 7:33, 173, 190, 191, 9:1, 3, 4, 5, 6, 7, 17, 28, 33, 36, 113, 10:18, 28, 105, 11:54, 12:38, 13:36, 106, 128, 14:22, 15:94, 16:1, 3, 35, 54, 86, 18:26, 36, 42, 100, 110, 120, 123, 20:32, 22, 17, 26, 31, 23:59, 92, 24:3, 35, 27:59, 63, 28:68, 82, 29:8, 65, 30:31, 33, 35, 40, 42, 31:13, 15, 33:73, 39:65, 67, 40:12, 42, 73, 84, 41:6, 42:13, 48:6, 52:43, 59:23, 60:12, 61:9, 72:2, 20,98:1,6

Assuring Muhaymin مهيمن

Confirming the book that was before it and assuring it (5:48)

See also 59:23

Asylum Mahis محيص

Those who dispute concerning our signs may know they have no asylum (42:35)

See also, 4:121, 14:21, 41:48, 50:36

Attribute Da'a دعا See Call

Attribute vt Daa دعا See Call

Augur ill vt Ittayyara إطَّير

We augur ill of those that are with thee (27:47)

See also 7:131, 36:18

Avarice Shuhh شح

Souls are very prone to avarice (4:128)

See also, 59:9, 64:16

Award Jaza جزاء See Recompense

Away Hayhat هيهات

Away with that which you are promised (23:36)

Azar Azar آزر

And when Abraham said to his father Azar (6:74)

B

Babylon Babil بابل

> That which was sent down upon Babylon's two angels (2:102)

Backbite vt Ightaba اغتاب

> Do not spy, neither backbite one another (49:12)

Backbiter Hammaz, Humazah هماز، همزه See Slanderer

Bad Khabith خبيث See Corrupt.

Badr Badr بدر

> God most surely helped you at Badr (3:123)

Bahira Bahirah (A camel dedicated to idols) بحيرة

> Idols, such as Bahira (5:103)

Balance Mizan ميزان See Scales.

Band Shirdhimah شرزمة See Troop

Baptism Sibghah صبغة

> Who is there that baptizes fairer than God? (2:138)

Barbarian Ajamiy أعجمى See Non-Arab

Barrea Safsaf صفصف See Level

Barren Aqim (M) Aqir (F) عقيم ، عاقر

> He makes whom He will barren (42:50)
> Shall I have a son, seeing my wife is barren, (19:8)
> See also 22:55, 51:29,41
> For Aqir 3:40,19:5

Barrier Barzakh برزخ

He set between them a barrier (25:53)
See also 23:100, 55:20

Battle Ba's بأس See Might

Battlements A'raf اعراف See Ramparts

Be a hypocrite vt Nafaqa نافق

That He might also know the hypocrites and the true believers (3:167)
The Bedouins are more stubborn in unbelief and hypocrisy (9:97)
See also, 4:61, 88, 138, 140, 142, 145, 8:49, 9:64, 67, 68, 73, 101, 29:11, 12, 24, 48, 60, 73, 48:6, 57:13, 59:11, 63:1, 7, 8, 66:9

Be an agressor I'tada إعتدى See Commit Transgression

Be blind vt Amiya' عمي

But blind are the hearts within the breasts (22:46)
See also 5:71, 6:104, 28:66

Be Charitable TaSadaqa تصدق See Give free will offering

Be corrupted Fasada فسد

The heavens and the earth and whosoever in them had surely corrupted (23:71)
See also 2:251, 21:22

Be importune Ahfa احفى See Press

Be insolent Bagha بغى

Fight the insolentone till it reverts to God's commandment (49:9)
Shall I seek after a Lord other than God (6:164)

Your insolence is only against yourselves (10:23)
See also, 2:90,173, 213, 3:19,83,99,4:34, 5:50,6:145, 146, 164, 7:33, 45, 86, 140, 9:47, 10:23, 90, 11:19, 12:63, 14:3, 16:90, 115, 18:64, 108, 22:60, 28:76, 77, 38:22, 24, 42:14, 27, 39, 42, 45:17, 49:55:20

Be lost Dalla ضل See Astray

Be miser Bakhil بخل See Be niggardly

Be niggardly Bakhila بخل

Whosoever is niggardly is niggardly only to his own soul (47:38)
Such as are niggardly, and bid men to be niggardly (57:24)
See also 3:180, 4:37,9:76,47:37,57:24,92:8

Be Right Sadaqa صدق See Speak truth

Be Sincere Sadaqa صدق See Speak truth

Be thankless vt Kaffara كفر See Disblieve

Be true Sadaqa صدق See Speak truth

Be watchful Hafaza حافظ

Be watchful over your way of prayers (2:238)
See also, 6:92,23:9,70:34

Bear Hamala حمل

How many a beast that bears not its own provision. (29:60)
God knows what every female bears (13:8)
See also 2:248, 286, 6:146, 7:176, 189, 9:92, 11:14, 12:36, 13:8, 16:7, 27, 17:3, 70, 19:2, 27, 58, 20:100, 111, 122:2, 23, 122 29:12, 13, 60, 31:14, 33:72, 35:11, 18,

36:41, 40:7, 80, 41:47, 46:15, 51:2, 54:13, 62:5, 65:48, 69:11, 17

Bearer of good tidings Bashir بشير

I am only a warner, and a bearer of good tidings (7:188)
There has come to you a bearer of good tidings (5:19)
See also, 2:119, 5:19, 11:2, 12:96, 34:28, 35:24, 41:4

Beast Bahimah بهيمة

Permitted to you is the beast of the flocks (5:1)
That they may mention God's name over such beasts of the flocks (22:34)
See also 22:28

Beast Dabbah دابة

God has created every beast of water (24:45)
The worst of beasts in God's sight are those that are deaf (8:22)
To God bows every thing in the heavens, and every creature crawling (16:49)
See also 2:164, 6:38, 8:55, 11:56, 16:61, 22:18, 24:45, 27:82, 29:60, 31:10, 34:14, 35:28, 45, 42:29, 45:4

Beasts of sacrifice Budn بـدن

Beasts of sacrifice — We have appointed them (22:36)

Become Jew Hada هاد See Judaise

Become learned Tafqqaha تفقه

Why should not a party of every section of them go forth, to become learned in religion (9:122)

Bedouins A'rab اعراب See Nomads

Beggar Qani قاني

When their flanks collapse, eat of them and feed the beggar and the suppliant (22:36)

Begin Bada'a بدأ See Originate

Bekka Bakka (A name for Mecca) بكة

First House established for the people was that at Bekka (3:96)

Believe v.t. Amana امن

We believe in God and the Last Day (2:8)

O believers, eat of the good things, (2:172)

See also, 2:9, 13, 14, 25, 26, 62, 78, 82, 103, 104, 126, 136, 137, 153, 165, 172, 177, 178, 183, 208, 212, 213, 214, 218, 248, 253, 254, 257, 264, 267, 277, 278, 282,285, 3:7,16,52,53,57

Believe vt. Sadaqa صدق See Confirm

Believers Muminun المومنون

Fear God, 3:102

To fear nothing else, 10:67

Hold together, 3:103

Enjoin right and forbid wrong, 3: 104, 110

Protected from harm, 3:111, 5:105

Protected by angels, 41:30-31

Warned against Unbelievers, 3:118-120, 196, 9:23-24, 60:13

Their lives sacred, 4:92-93

Not to slight those who salute, 4:94

If weak and oppressed, 4:97-100

Not to sit where God's signs are ridiculed, 44:140, 6:68

To prefer Believers for friends, 4:144, 5:57-58

Witness to fair dealing, 5:8

Duties of God, 5:35, 66:8

Not to ask questions, 5:101-102
Grades of dignity, 8:4
Described, 8:24,9:71,111-112,10:104-106,12:20-24, 28-29,231-11,57-61,28:53,32:15-17:42:36-39, 49:7, 15
To be firm, 8:45
To obey and not lose heart, 8:46
Not to be weary and faint-hearted. 47:35
Affection between their hearts, 8:63
To conquer against odds, 8:65-66
Adopt exile, fight for God, 8:72, 74-75
Help and give asylum, 8:72
Ask for no exemption from danger, 9:43-45
Protect each other, 9:71
Rejoice in their bargain, 9:111, 61:10-11
To be with those true in word and deed, 9:119
To study and teach, 9:122
Will be established in strength, 14:27
To practice prayer and charity, 14:31
To say what is best, 17:53-55
To be heirs, to inherit Paradise, 23:10-11
Promise to, 29:55-57
Manners, 24:62-63
Evil will be blotted out from, 29:7
Their ills removed, 47:2
Conduct, 33:69-71, 48:29
Prayer for them by those round Throne of God, 40:7-9
Believers fear God, 3:102
Warned against Unbelievers, 3:118-120, 196, 9:23-24, 60:13
To fear nothing else 10:67
Protected by angels, 41:30-31
To make peace, 49:9
To avoid suspicion and spying, 49:12

Not to despair or exult, 57:23
To remember God in humility, 57:16

Beneficent Barr بر See Pious

Benefit Ala الى See Bounty

Benificent Rahman رحمن See All-merciful

Be patient vt Sabara صبر See Endure patiently

Bestower Wahhab وهاب See All-giver

Betray Khana خان

O believers, betray not God and the Messenger (8:27)
Surely God loves not the treacherous (12:52)
See also 4:10, 55, 17:97, 22:4, 25:11, 31:21, 33:64, 34:12, 35:6, 48:13, 67:5, 10, 11, 76:4, 84:12

Be watchful Hafaza حافظ

Be watchful over the prayers (2:238)
See also 6:92, 23:9, 70:34

Bid to Amara آمر See Command

Bind Ghalla غل See Defraud

Birds Ababil أبابيل

And He loosed upon them birds in flight (105:3)

Bitter cold Zamharir زمهرير

Therein they shall see neither sun nor bitter cold (76:13)

Bitter Ujaj أجاج

Were it Our will, we would make it bitter (56:70)
See also 25:53, 35:12

Black smoke Yahmum يحموم

And the shadow of a smoking blaze (56:43)

Blame Junah جناح See Fault

Blaze Sa'ir سعير

> A party in Paradise, and a party in the Blaze (42:7)
> We have prepared for the unbelievers chains, fetters, and a Blaze (76:4)
> See also 4:10, 55, 17:97, 22:4, 25:11, 31:21, 33:64, 34:12, 35:6, 48:13, 67:5, 10, 11, 76:4, 84:12

Blazing Wahhaj وهاج

> We appointed a blazing lamp (78:13)

Blind A'ma أعمى

> Are the blind and the seeing man equal? (6:50)
> Thou shall not guide the blind out of their error (27:81)
> See also, 2:18, 171, 10:43,11:24,13:16,19,17:72,97, 20:124, 125, 24:61, 27:73, 30:53, 35:19, 40:58, 43:40, 48:17,80:2

Blood Dam دم

> Between filth and blood: pure milk, sweet to drinkers (16:66)
> The flesh of them shall not reach God, neither their blood (22:37)
> Forbidden to you are carrion, blood (5:3)
> You shall not shed your own blood (2:84)
> See also, 2:30,173,6:145,7:133,12:18.16:115

Blood wit Diyah دية

> And blood-wit is to be paid to his family (4:92)

Blood-clot Alaqah علقة

> Created man of a blood-clot (96:2)

See also, 22:55, 51:29, 41

Boal Ba'l (A pre-Islamic deity) بعل

    Do you call upon Boal? (37:125)

Bonds 'Aqd عقد

    O believers, fulfil your bonds (5:1)

Book Kitab كتاب

    Book of records of deeds, 18:49, 36:12, 54:52-53
    Book (Revelation), is guidance sure, 2:2
    To be studied 2:121
    (Qur'an) verses fundamental and allegorical 3:7
    (Qur'an), light and guide, 5:15-16
    People of the, 3:64-80, 98-99, 113-115, 187, 199, 4:47, 153-161
    Appeal to people of the 5:59-60, 68
    Their hypocrisy 5:61:63
    Forgiven if they had stood fast to their lights, 5:66
    Know but refuse to believe, 6:20
    Mother or foundation of the, 3:7, 13:39, 43:4
    For each period 13:38
    On blessed Night, 44:3-4
    From God, 46:2

Booty Ghanima, Maghanam غنيمة ، مغانم

    Eat of what you have taken as booty (8:69)
    See also 8:41
    For Maghnam 4:94, 48:15, 19, 20

Bottom (of a well or pit) Ghayabah غيابة

    Kill not Joseph, but cast him into the bottom of the pit (12:10)
    See also 12:15

Boundary Muntaha منتهى See Final end

Bounds Hudud حدود

> Those are God's bounds:Keep well within them(2:187)
> Those are God's bounds; do not transgress them (2:229)
> See also 2:229,230, 4:13,14,9:97,112, 58:4, 65:1

Bounty Ala الى

> Remember God's bounties (7:69)
> Which of your Lord's bounties will you deny? (55:77)
> See also 7:74, 53:55, 55:13, 16, 18, 21, 23, 25, 28, 30, 32, 34, 36, 38, 40, 42, 45, 47, 49, 51, 53, 55, 57, 59, 61, 63, 65, 67, 69, 71, 73, 75

Bow down vt Sjada سجد

> To God bow all who are in the heavens and the earth (13:15)
> The stars and the trees bow themselves (55:6)
> See also, 2:34, 58, 125, 3:43, 113, 4:102, 154, 7:11, 12, 120, 161, 206, 9:112, 12:4, 100, 13:1, 15:29, 30, 31, 32, 33, 98, 16:48, 49, 17:61, 107, 18:50, 19:58, 20:70, 116, 22:18, 26, 77, 25:60 64, 26:46, 219, 27:24, 25, 32:15, 38:72, 73, 75, 39:9, 41:37, 49:29, 50:40, 53:62, 55:6, 53:62, 68:42, 43, 76:26, 84:21, 96:19

Bow vt Rakaa ركع See Prostrate one self

Break the head Damagha دمغ See Prevail Over

Breast Sadr صدر

> Lord, open my breast (20:25)
> God knows the thoughts in the breast (3:154)
> Thy Lord knows what their hearts conceal and what they publish. (27:74)

See also, 3:29, 118, 119, 154, 4:90, 517, 6:125, 7:2,43, 8:43, 10:57, 11:5, 12, 15:47, 97, 16:106, 17:51, 20:25, 22:46, 27:74, 28:69, 29:10, 49, 31:23, 35:38,39:7, 22, 40:19, 56, 80, 42:24, 57:6,59:9, 13, 64:4, 67:13,94:1, 100:10, 114:5

Bring Halumma هلم See Come

Bring to Ata أعطى See Give

Brother Akh أخ

By His blessing you became brothers. (3:103)
The believers indeed are brothers, (59:10)
See also, 2:178, 220,3:156, 168, 4:11,12, 23, 176, 5:25, 30, 31, 6:87, 7:65, 73,85, 111, 142, 150, 151, 202,9:11, 23, 24, 10:87, 11:50, 61, 84, 12:5, 7, 8, 58, 59, 63, 64, 65, 69, 70, 76, 77, 87, 89, 90, 100, 15:47, 17:27, 19:53, 20:30, 42, 23:45, 24:31, 61, 25:35, 26:36, 106, 124, 142, 161, 27:45, 28:34, 35, 29:36, 33:5, 18, 55, 38:23, 46:21, 49:10, 12, 50:13, 58:22, 59:10, 11, 70:12, 80:34

Burden Isr اصر See Load

Burden Isr إصر See Load

Burning Hariq حريق

Taste the chastisement of the burning (3:181)
See also 8:50,22:9,22,85:10

Burning wind Samum سموم

God was gracious to us and guarded us against the chastisement of the burning wind 52:27
See also 15:27,56:42

C

Call Da'wah دعوة

    I am near to answer the call (2:186)
    What you call me to, has heard no call (40:43)
    See also 10:89, 13:14, 14:44, 30:25

Call vt Da'a دعا

    I am near to answer the call of the caller, who he calls to Me (2:186)
    When they embark in the ships, they call on God (29:65)
    And do not call apart from God (10:106)
    See also 2:23, 61,68, 69, 70, 186, 171, 186 260, 282, 221, 2:23, 38, 61, 104, 153, 4:117, 6:40, 41, 52, 56, 63, 71, 108, 7:29, 37,55, 56, 134, 180 189, 193, 194 195, 197, 198, 8:24, 10:12, 22,25, 38, 66, 106, 11:13, 62, 101, 12:33, 108, 13:14,36, 14:9,10,22,39, 40, 16:20, 86, 125, 17:11, 52, 56, 57 67, 71,110, 18:14, 24, 28, 57, 19:4, 48, 91, 20:108, 21:90, 22:12, 13,62,67,73, 23:73, 117, 48, 51, 63, 25:13, 14, 68, 77, 26:72, 213, 27:62, 80, 28:25, 41, 64, 87,88, 29:42, 65, 30, 30:25, 33,52, 31:21, 30, 32, 32:16, 33:5, 34:22, 35:6, 13, 14, 18, 40, 37:125, 38:51, 39:8, 38, 49, 40:10,14, 20, 26, 41, 42, 43, 49, 50, 60, 65, 66, 74, 41:5, 33, 48, 49, 51, 42:13, 15, 43:49, 86, 44:22, 55, 45:28, 46:4,5, 31,32, 47:35, 38, 48:16, 52:28, 54:8,8, 10, 57:8, 61:7,68:42, 43, 70:17, 71:5, 6, 7,8, 72:18, 19, 20, 84:1, 96:17, 18

Calumny Buhtan بهتان See Slander

Calumny Ifk افك See Slander

Camel (she) Naqah ناقة

> This is the she-camel of God to be a sign for you (11:64)
> See also 7:733,77,17:59, 26:155,54:27,91:13

Camel Bair بعير

> We shall obtain an extra camel's load (12:65)
> See also, 12:72

Camel Ibil, Jamal ابل، جمل

> Do they not consider how the camel was created (88:17)
> See also 6:144,7:40,77:33

Caprice Hawa هوى See Desire

Captive Asir أسير

> If they come to you as captives, you reason them (2:85)
> They give food, for the love of Him, to the needy, the orphan, the captive (76:8)
> It is not for any Prophet to have prisoners. (8:67)
> See also, 8:70

Carry Hamala حمل See Bear

Carve vt Nahata نحت See Hew

Cast down Gadda غض

> Say to the believers that they cast down their eyes (24:30)
> See also 24:31,49:3

Cast Vt. Rama رمى See Throw

Cattle Naam نعام

> Surely in the cattle there is a lesson for you (23:21)
> It is God who appointed for you the cattle (40:79)
> See also 3:14, 4:119, 5:1,95, 6:136, 138, 139, 142, 7:179, 10:24, 16:5, 66, 80, 20:54, 22:28, 30, 34, 23:21, 25:44,

49, 26:133, 32:27, 35:28, 36:71, 39:6, 40:79, 41:11, 43:12, 47:12, 79:33, 80:32

Cause of sin Aththama أثم

>Wherein is no idle talk, no cause of sin (52:23)
>See also 56:25

Cause of sin Tathim تأثيم

>Wherein is no idle talk, no cause of sin (52:23)
>See also 56:25

Cause to go astray Adalla أضل See Lead astray

Cave Kahf كهف

>Take refuge in the cave for three hundred years (18:25)
>See also 18:9, 10, 11, 17

Cease v.t. Fataa فتئ

>Thou wilt never cease mentioning Joseph till thou art consumed (12:85)

Change Ghayyara غير

>God changes not what is in a people (13:11)
>See also, 4:119, 8:53, 13:11

Change Tahwil تحويل

>Thou will find no change to Our wont (17:77)
>See also 17:56, 35:43

Chant vt Rattala رتل

>We have chanted it very distinctly (25:32)
>See also 73:4

Chapter of the Koran Surah سورة See Sura

Character Khluq خلق See Morality

Charge Kallafa كلف

> God charges no soul save to its capacity (2:286)
> God charges no soul save with what He has given him (65:7)
> See also 21:233, 4:84, 6:152, 7:42, 23:62

Charger Adiyah عادية

Charity Maun ماعون

> And refuse charity (107:7)

Charity Sadqah صدقة See Freewill offering

Chastise v.t. Adhdhaba عذب

> He forgives whom He will and chastises whom He will (3:129)
> See also 2:284, 3:56, 128, 4:173, 5:18, 40, 115, 188, 7:164, 8:33, 9:14, 26, 39, 55, 66, 74, 85, 101, 106,17:15,54, 58, 18:86, 87, 20:47, 27:21, 29:21, 33:24, 48:6, 14, 16, 17,25,58:8,59:3,65:8,88:24,89:25,34:35, 37:59

Chastisement Adhab عذاب See Punishment

Chastisement Nakal نكال

Cheek Khadd خد

> Turn not thy cheek away from men in scorn (31:18)

Chest Sadr صدر See Breast

Chin Adhqan اذقان

> We have put on their necks fetters up to the chin (36:8)
> See also 17:107, 109

Choking Ghussah غصة

> Food that chokes and a painful chastisement (73:13)

Christ Masih مسيح See Jesus

Christian Nasrani نصراني

> Abraham in truth was not a Jew neither a Christian (3:67) See also, 2:62, 11, 113, 120, 135, 140, 5:14, 18, 51, 69, 82, 9:30 22:17

Christian priest Qissis قسيس

> Because some of them are priests and monks, and they are not proud (5:82)

Church Biya بيعة

> There had been destroyed cloisters and churches (22:40)

Circumambulate vt Tafa طاف See Go round

Clamorous Sarsar صرصار

> We loosened against them a wind clamorous in days of ill fortune 41:16
> See also 54:19, 69:6

Clan 'Ashirah عشيرة

> Warn thy clan, thy nearest kin
> See also 9:24, 58:22.

Cleanse vt Zakka زكى See Purify

Cleave v.t. Infalaqa انفلق

> It cleaved and each part was as a mighty mount (26:63)

Clement Afuf عفوف See All-pardoning

Clinging Lazib لازب

> We created them of clinging clay (37:11)

Clot Alaqah علقة See Blood clot

Clothing Libas لباس See Garment

Cloud Muzn مزن

> Did you send it down from the clouds, or did We send it? (56:69)

Codex Imam امام See Leader

Colour Sibghah صبغة See Baptism

Column 'Imad عماد See Pillar

Come Halumma هلم

> Come to us and come to battle (33:18)

Come Hayta هيت

> Come she said take me (12:23)

Coming of age Ashudd أشد

> Thy Lord desired that they should come of age. (18:82)
> When he was fully grown, We gave him judgment and knowledge (12:22)
> See also, 6:152, 17:34, 22:5, 28:14, 40:67, 46:15

Commit Transgression I'tada إعتدى

> Those are God's bounds; do not transgress them (2:229)
> Do not retain them by force, to transgress (2:231)
> See also 2:61, 65, 178, 190, 194, 3:112, 5:2, 78, 87, 94, 107, 6:119, 7:55, 9:10, 10:74, 50:25, 68:12, 83:12

Command Kalimah كلمة See Word

Command vt Amara أمر

> My Lord has commanded justice (7:29)
> Evil is the thing your faith bids you to. (2:93)

I am commanded to surrender to the Lord of all being (40:66)

See also, 2:27, 44,67, 68,93, 109, 117, 169, 210, 222, 268, 275, 3:21,47, 80, 104, 109, 110, 111, 114, 128, 147,152,154,159,186,4:37,47,58,59,60,83, 114, 119, 5:52, 95, 117, 6:8, 58, 159, 7:12, 28, 29, 54, 77, 110, 145, 154, 199, 8:42, 43, 44, 9:31, 50, 67, 71, 106, 112, 123, 12:15, 18, 21, 32, 40, 41, 68, 83, 102, 13:2, 112, 25,31,36, 14:22, 32, 15:66, 16:12, 12, 33, 76, 77, 90, 17:16, 85, 18:10, 16,21, 28, 50, 69, 73, 82, 88, 19:21,35,39,55,64, 20:26, 32, 62, 90, 93, 132, 21:73, 81, 93,22:41,65,67,76,23:27, 53, 24:21, 53, 62, 63, 25:60, 26:35, 151, 27:32, 33, 91 ,28:44, 30:4, 25, 46, 31:17, 22, 32:5, 24, 33:36, 37, 38, 34:12, 35, 35:4, 36:82, 38:36, 40:15, 44, 66, 68, 78, 39:11, 12, 64, 41:12, 42:11, 38, 43, 52, 53, 43:79, 44:4, 5, 45 :12, 17, 18, 46:25, 47:21, 26, 49:7, 9, 51:4, 44, 52:32, 54:3, 12, 50, 57:5, 14, 24, 59:15, 64:5, 65:1, 3, 4, 5, 8, 9, 12, 66:6, 74:5, 82:19, 97:4, 98:5

Commerce Tijarah تجارة See Merchandise

Commerce Tijarah تجارة

Look for commerce that comes not to naught (35:29)
What is with God is better than diversion and merchandise (62:11)
See also 2:16, 282,4:29,9:24,24:37,61:10,62:11

Commit adultery Zana زنا See Fornicate

Commit ungodliness Fasaqa فسق

We seized the evildoers with evil chatisement for their ungodliness 2:167)
See also 2:26, 59,99, 3:82,110, 5:3, 25, 26, 47, 49, 59, 81, 108, 6:49 121, 145, 7:102,145,163,165,9:8, 24, 53, 67, 80,

84, 96, 18:50, 21:74, 24:4, 55, 27:12, 28:32, 29:34, 32:18, 20, 43:54, 46:20, 35, 49:6, 7, 11, 51:46, 57:16, 26, 27, 59:5, 19, 61:5, 63:6

Common folk Ummy أمي See Illiterate

Community Ummah أمة See Nation

Compact 'Aqd عقد See Bond

Compact Mithaq ميثاق

>for their breaking their compact We cursed them (5:13) See Also 2:27, 63, 83, 84, 93, 3:81, 187, 4:21, 90, 92, 154, 155, 517, 12, 13, 14, 70, 7:169, 8:72, 13:20, 25, 33:7, 57:8

Companion Rafiq رفيق

>Just men, martyrs, the righteous: good companions are they (4:69)

Company Fi'ah فئة See Host

Comparable Kufu' كفو See Equal

Compassionate Awwah أواه

>Abraham was a compassionate clement (9:114)
>See also 11:75

Compares Andad انداد

>So set not up compares to God knowingly (2:22)
>See also 2:165, 14:30, 34:33, 39:8, 41:9

Compel against Sakhkhara سخر See Subject

Compensate Aslaha أصلح See Make amends

Comprehend 'Aqala عقل See Understand

Conceal Akhfa أخفى

Yet I know very well what you conceal and what you publish (60:1)
If you conceal them, and give them to the poor, that is better for you (2:271)
See also 2:284, 3:29, 118, 154, 4:149, 5:15, 6:28, 91, 14:38, 20:15, 24:31, 27:25, 32:17, 33:37, 54, 40:19

Conceal Katama كتم

Do not conceal the testimony (2:283)
Do not conceal the truth knowingly (2:42)
And God disclosed what you were hiding (2:72)
See also 2:33, 146, 159, 174, 228, 283, 3:71, 167, 187, 4:37, 42, 5:61, 99, 106, 21:110, 24:29, 40:28

Confer on someone Abla أبلى

That He might confer on the believers a fair benefit (8:17)

Confirm vt Saddaqa صدق

Thou hast confirmed the vision (37:105)
Who confirm the Day of Doom (70:26)
See also 2141, 89, 91, 97, 101, 3:33, 39, 50, 81, 4:47, 5:46, 48, 6:97, 10:37, 12:111, 28:34, 34:20, 35:31, 37:37, 52, 39:33, 46:12, 30, 56:57, 61:6, 66:12, 70:26, 75:31, 92:6

Conquer Ghalaba غلب See Overcome

Consider Tadabbar تدبر See ponder

Consolation Shura شورى

Constellation Buruj برج See Tower

Consult v.t. Itamara ائتمر

And consult together honourably (65:6)
See also 28:20

Consumer Akkal اكال See Greedy

Continuous torment Gharam غرام

Its chastisment is torment most terrible (25:65)

Convenant 'Ahd عهد

Fulfil God's convenant (17:34)
See also, 2:27, 40, 80, 100, 124, 177, 3:76, 77, 7:109, 8:56, 9:4, 7, 12, 111, 112, 13:20, 25, 16:91, 95, 19:78, 87, 20:86, 23:8, 33:15, 70:32

Copious Ghadaq غدق

We would give them to drink of water copious (72:16)

Corrupt Bur بور

You thought evil thoughts and you were a people corrupt (48:12)
See also 25:18

Corrupt Khabith خبيث

Do not exchange the corrupt for the good (4:2)
That God may distinguish the corrupt from the good (8:37)
See also 2:267, 3:179, 5:100, 8:37, 14:26

Corruption Dakhal دخل See Mutual deceit

Corruption Fasad فساد

God loves not corruption (2:205)
God loves not the workshop of corruption (5:64)
See also 5:32,33,64,8:73,11:116,28:77,83,30:41, 40:26,89:12

Couch Arikah أريكة

    Therein they shall recline upon couches (76:13)
    See also 18:31,36:56, 83:23,35

Council Mala ملأ

    Whenever a council of his people passed by him they scoffed at him (11:38)
    See also 2:246, 7:60, 66, 75,88, 90, 103, 127, 10:75, 83,88, 11:27, 97, 12:43, 23:24,33,46, 26:34, 37:29,32, 38, 28:20,32,38,37:8, 38:6, 69,43:46

Counsel Shura شورى

    Perform the prayer, their affair being counsel between them (42:38)

Counsel Shura شورى

    Perform the prayer, their affair being counsel between them (42:38)

Count Ah'sa أحصى See Number

Counterpoise Adl عدل

    No counterpoise shall be accepted from it (2:123)
    See also, 2:48, 282, 4:58, 5:95, 106, 6:70, 115, 16:76, 90, 49:9, 65:2

Courser, Adiyah عادية

    By the snorting chargers (100:1)

Covering Ghishawah غشاوة See Veil

Coverings Akinnah أكنه See Veils

Crashing Hadd هد See Demolition

Crawling creature Dabbah دابة See Beast

Create vt Khalaqa خلق

O you men, serve your Lord who created you (2:21)
I have not created jinn and mankind except to serve me (51:56)
See also, 2:29, 228, 3:59, 191, 4:1, 5:18, 6:1, 2, 75, 94, 100, 7:11, 12, 54, 181, 185, 189, 9:36, 10:3,5,6,11:7,119, 15:16, 14:19, 32, 15:26, 27, 33, 85, 16:4, 5, 48, 70, 81, 17:61, 70, 99, 18:37, 48, 19:9, 67, 20:4, 55, 21:16, 33, 22:5, 23:12, 14, 17, 91, 115, 24:45, 25:2, 49, 54, 59, 26:78, 116, 185, 27:60, 29:44, 61, 30, 8, 20, 21, 40, 54, 31, 10, 11, 25, 32, 4, 7, 35:11, 40, 36:36, 42, 71, 77, 81, 37:11, 96, 150, 38:27, 75, 76, 39:5, 6, 38, 40:67, 41:9, 15, 21, 37, 43:9, 12, 87, 44:38, 39, 45:122, 46:3, 4, 33, 49:13, 50:16, 38, 51:49, 56, 52:36, 53:45, 54:49, 55:3, 14, 15, 56:57, 57:4, 64:2, 3, 65:12, 67:2, 3, 14, 70, 39, 71:14, 15, 74:11, 75:38, 76:2, 28, 78:8, 80:18, 19, 82:7, 87:2, 90:4, 92:3, 95:4, 96:1, 2, 113:2

Create Dhara'a ذرع See Scatter

Creation Fitrah فطرة See Original

Creation Khalq خلق

God commands 'Be and it is, 2:117,16:40,36:82,40:68 54:50
In six periods 7:54, 32:4, 57:4
Begins and repeated 10:4, 27:64, 29:19-20.
A new 13:5, 14:48, 17:49, 98; 21:104, 35:16
For just ends, 15:85,16:3, 44:39, 45:22, 46:3
Does obedience to God, 16:48-50
Not for sport 21:16-17
40:68, 54:50

Of man, 23:12-14,
Variety in 35:27-28
In true proportions 39:5
Of heaven and earth greater than creation of man, 40:57
Purpose of 51:56-58

Crime Dhand ذنب See Also Sin

Crime Ma'arrah معرة
There befall you guilt unwittingly (48:25)

Criterion Furqan فرقان See Salvation

Crumbling Har هار See Weak

Crush vt Damdama دمدم
So their Lord crushed them for their sin, and levelled them (9:14)

Cunning 'Alim عليم See All-knowing

Curtain Hijab حجاب See Veil

Curving, Amt أمت
Wherein those will see no crookedness neither any curving (20:107)

Cusions Namariq نمارق
And cusions arrayed (88:15)

Customary action Sunnah سنة See Institution

D

Damned Rajim رجيم See Accursed

Dark A 'ma أعمى See Blind

Date-spot Naqir نقير

    They do not give the people a single date-spot (4:43)
    See also 4:124

David Dawud داؤد

    Fights Goliath 2:251
    Given psalms 4:163
    Of Nuh's seed 6:84
    Mountains subjected to him 21:79, 34:10
    He was examined 34:24

Death Maut موت

    Death by God's leave 3:145
    Inevitable 3:185, 4:78
    Confusion of the wicked 6: 93-94
    Angels reproach Unbelievers, 8:50-54
    In death the transgressor will not die, 14:7, 20:74, 87:13,
    For wrong doers, 16:28-29
    For righteous 16:30-32
    Taste of it 3:185, 21:35 29:57
    First 37:59
    Not the end of all things 45:24-26
    And changed from thereafter 56:60-61
    Scene at it 56:83-87 75:26-29
    Sincere men flee not from death 62:6-8

Debt Dayn دين

    After any bequest he may bequeath of any debt (4:11)

See also 2:282, 4:12

Debtor Gharim غريم

>Those whose hearts are brought together, the ransoming of slaves, debtors (9:60)

Deceive vt Gharra غرّ See Delude

Deceiver Gharur غرور

>Let not the Deluder delude you concerning God (31:33)
>See also, 35:5, 57:14

Deception Gharur غرور See Delusion

Deck Tabarraja تبرّج See Display

Declare Bayyana بين See Make clear, manifest

Declare Haddatha حدث See Tell

Defend Dafa'a دفع

>God will defend those who believe (22:38)

Defend vt 'Asama عصم

>Who is he that shall defend you from God (33:17)
>Today there is no defender from God's command (11:43)
>God will protect thee from men (5:67)
>See also 10:27, 11:43, 40:33

Defer Akhkhara أخّر

>A soul shall know what it has sent before and what it has done (82:5)
>He is defering them to a stated term (35:45)
>God's term, when it comes, cannot be defered (71:4)
>See also 4:77, 11:8, 104, 14:10,42, 44, 16:61, 17:62, 63:10,11, 71:4

Defraud Ghalla غل

> Whose defrauds shall bring the fruits (3:161)
> It is not for a Prophet to be defraudulent (3:161)
> See also 3:161, 5:64, 17:29, 69:30

Degree Darajah درجة See Rank

Delay Fawaq فواق

> These are only awaiting for a single cry, to which there is no delay (38:15)

Deliver vt Najja نجى

> Who delivers you from the shadows of land and sea? (6:13)
> My Lord, deliver me and my people from that they do (26:169)
> See also 2:49, 6:64, 7:89, 10:37, 86, 92, 103, 11:58, 66, 94, 12:110, 15:59, 17:69, 19:72, 20:40, 21:71, 47, 76, 88, 23:28, 26:118, 170, 28:21, 29:32, 33, 65, 31:32, 37:76, 115, 134, 39:61, 41:18, 44:30, 54:34, 66:11

Deliverance Balagh بلاغ

> It is for thee only to deliver the message (42:48)
> Thine it is only to deliver the manifest message (16:82)
> See also 3:20, 5:92, 99, 13:40, 14:52, 16:52, 16:35, 21:106, 24:54, 29:18, 36:17, 46:35, 64:12, 72:23

Deliverer Fattah فتاح

> He is the Deliverer, the All-knowing (34:26)

Delude vt Gharra غر

> The lies they forged has deluded them (3:24)
> See also 6:70, 130, 7:51, 8:49, 45:35, 57:14, 82:6

Deluder Gharur غرور See Deceiver

Delusion Gharur غرور

> The present life is but the joy of delusion (3:185)
> See also 4:120, 6:112, 7:22, 17:64, 33:12, 35:40, 57:20, 67:20

Demolition Hadd هد

> The mountains well nigh fall down crashing (19: 90)

Deny Kaffara كفر See Disbelieve

Deny vt Ankara أنكر

> They recognise the blessing of God, then they deny it (16:83)
> Their hearts deny and they are puffed up with pride (16:22)
> See also 3:104, 110, 114, 5:79, 7:157, 9:67, 71, 112, 12:58, 13:36, 15:62, 16:83, 90, 21:50, 22:41, 72, 23:69, 24:21, 29:29, 45, 31:17, 40:81, 51:25, 58:2

Deposit Amanah أمانة See Trust

Deprived Mahrum محروم See Outcast

Desire Bagha بغى See Be insolent

Desire Hawa هوى

> Do not follow the caprices of those who cried lies (6:150)
> See also 2:120, 145, 4:135, 5:48, 4977, 6:56, 119, 150, 7:176, 13:37, 18:28, 20:16, 23:71, 25:43, 28:50, 30:29, 38:26, 42:15, 45:18, 23, 47:14, 53:3, 54:3, 79:40

Desire Shahwah شهوة See Lust

Desolate Safasaf صفصف See Level

Desperate Qanut قنوط

When evil visits him, he is cast down and desperate (41:49)

Despise Ahana أهان See Abase

Destroy Ahlaka أهلك

Never a city We destroyed, but it had awareness (26:28)
We destroyed them because of their Sins (6:6)
How many a city We have destroyed that flourished insolent ease (28:58)

See also 2:205, 3:117, 5:17, 6:6, 26,131, 7:4,129, 155, 164, 173, 8:54, 9:42, 10:13, 11:117, 14:13, 15:4, 17:16, 17, 58, 18:59, 19:74, 98, 20:128, 134, 21:69, 95, 22:45,23:48, 26:139,208, 28:43,58, 59, 78, 29:31, 2:26, 36:31, 38:3, 43:8, 44:37, 45:24, 46:27, 50:36, 53:50, 4:51, 67:28, 77:16, 90:6

Destroy vt Damdama دمدم See Crush

Destruction Tahluka تهلكة See Perdition

Devil Gharur غرور See Deceiver

Devotional act Mansak منسك See Holy rite

Devout Taqiy تقى See God-fearing

Date-thread Fatil فتيل

They shall not be wronged a single date-thread (4:49)
See also 4:77, 17:71

Dhul Qarnain Dhul-Qarnayns ذو القرنين

O Dhul karnain, either thou shall chastise them (18:86)
See also, 18:83, 18:94

Dhul Kifl Dhul Kifl ذو الكفل

Idris, Dhul Kifl each was of the patient (21:85)

See also, 38:84

Dhul Nun Dhul Nun ذوالنون

> And Dhul Nun when he went forth enraged (21:87)

Difficulty 'Usr عسر See Hardship

Dinar Dinar دينار

> If thou trust him with one pound (3:75)

Direction of prayer Qiblah قبلة

> We did not appoint the direction thou wast facing(2:143)
> Make your houses a direction for men to pray to (10:87)
> See also 2:142,144,145

Direction Wijhah وجهة

> Every man has his direction to which he turns (2:148)

Dirham Dirham (A unit of currency, smaller than Dinar) درهم

> Then they sold him for a paltry price, a handful of counted dirhams (12:20)

Disbelieve vt Kaffara كفر

> I will set thy followers above the unbelievers (3:55)
> God has helped him already, when the unbelievers drove him forth (9:40)
> See also 2:6, 26,39, 89,102,105,126,161,171,212, 253,257,258,3:4,10, 12, 55, 56, 86, 90, 91, 97, 106, 116, 127, 149, 151, 156, 178, 196, 4:42, 51, 56, 76, 84, 89, 101, 102, 137, 167, 168, 5:3, 10, 12, 17, 36, 72, 73, 78, 80, 86, 103, 110, 6:17, 25, 7:66, 90, 8:12, 15, 30, 36, 38, 50, 52, 55, 59, 65, 73, 3:9, 26, 30, 37, 40, 54, 66, 74, 80, 84, 90, 10:4, 11:27, 27, 60, 68, 13:57, 27, 31, 32, 33, 43, 14:7, 9, 13, 18, 22, 15:12, 16:39, 84, 88, 106, 112, 17:69, 98, 18:37, 56, 102, 105, 106, 19:37, 73, 77, 21:30, 36, 39, 97,

22:19, 98, 18:37, 56, 102, 105, 106, 19:37, 73, 77, 21:30, 36, 39, 97, 22:19, 25, 55, 57, 72, 23, 24, 33, 24:39, 55, 57, 25:4, 32, 27:40, 67, 29:12, 23, 52, 30:16, 44, 58, 31:12, 23, 32:29, 33:25, 34:3, 7, 17, 31, 33, 43, 53, 25:7, 26, 36, 39, 36:47, 37:170, 28:2, 27

Discern 'Arafa عرف See Recognise

Disciple Hawariy حواري See Apostle

Disobey ' Asa عصى

Terrible angels who disobey not God (66:6)

Conspire not together in sin and enmity, and disobedience (58:9)

Who shall help me against God if I rebel? (11:63)

See also 2:62, 93, 3:112, 152, 4:14, 42, 46, 5:78, 6:15, 10:15, 91, 11:59, 63, 14:36, 18:69, 20:93, 121, 26:216, 33:36, 39:13, 49:7, 58:89, 60:12, 69:10, 71:21, 73:16 79:21

Disobey God's commandment Fasaqa فســـق See Commit ungodness

Disorder vt Afsada افسد See Do corruption

Display Tabarraja تبرج

Display not your finery, as did the pagans of old (33:33)
See also 24:60, 33:33

Disputation Hujjah حجة See Argument

Dissension Fitnah فتنة See Trial

Distinction Furqan فرقان See Salvation

Divine Law Shirah شرعة See Open Way

Do 'Amila عمل

Those who believe and do deeds (2:25)
All have degrees according to what they have done (6:132)
God is aware of the thing you do (3:180)
See also 2:62, 74, 82, 85, 96, 110, 134, 140 141, 233, 237, 265, 271, 277, 283, 3:30, 57, 4:17, 18, 57, 122, 123, 124, 128, 135, 173, 5:9,8, 62,66, 71, 93, 6:43, 54, 60, 88, 108, 122, 132, 7:42, 43, 53, 118, 129, 139, 147, 153, 180, 8:39, 47, 72, 9:9, 16, 94, 105, 121, 10:4, 9, 12, 14, 23, 41, 61, 11:11, 16, 23, 78, 52, 111, 112, 123, 12:19, 69, 13:29, 14:23, 42, 15:93, 16:28, 34, 93, 96, 97, 111, 119, 17:9, 84, 18:2, 30, 49, 79, 88,107, 110, 19:60, 96, 20:75, 82, 112, 21:27, 74, 82, 94, 22:14, 23,50, 56, 68, 23:51, 100, 24:24, 28, 38, 53, 55, 64, 26:112, 179, 188, 216, 227, 27:19, 84, 90, 93,28:67, 80, 84, 29:4, 7, 8, 9, 55, 58, 30:15, 41, 44, 45, 31:8, 15, 23, 29, 32:12, 14, 17, 35:2, 9, 31, 34,:4, 11,12,13, 25, 35, 37, 35:7, 37, 36:33, 54,71 37:39, 61, 96, 38:24, 28, 39:7, 35, 70, 40:40, 58, 41:8, 20, 22, 27, 33, 40, 46, 50, 42:22, 23, 26, 43:72, 45:15, 21, 28, 29,30, 35,46:14, 15, 16, 19, 47:2, 12, 48:11, 24, 29, 49:18, 52:16, 19, 53:31, 56:24, 57:4, 10, 58:3, 6,7,11, 13, 15, 59:18, 60:3, 62:8, 63:2, 11, 64:2, 7, 8, 9, 65:11, 66:7, 77:43, 84:25, 85:11, 95:6, 98:7, 99:7, 8, 103, 103:3

Do Corruption Afsada افسد

Do not corruption in the land (2:11)
See also 2:27, 30, 60, 205, 220, 3:63, 5:64,7:56,74, 86, 103, 127, 143, 10:40, 81, 91, 11:85, 12:73, 13:25, 16:88, 17:4, 26:152, 183, 27:14, 48, 28:4, 77, 29:30, 36, 38:28, 47:22

Do evil Zalama ظلم See Wrong

Do mischief vt Asa'a أساء

> Do not mischief in the earth, working corruption (26:183)
> See also 2:60, 7:74, 29:36

Do wrong Zalama ظلم See Wrong

Dog Star Shira شعري

> And that it is he who is the lord of Sirius (53:49)

Dominion Malakut ملكوت See Kingdom

Donate vt Tasaddqa تصدق See Give freewill offering

Dowry Faridah فريضة See Ordinance

Draw on gradually Istadraj استدرج

> We will draw then on little by little whence they know not (7:182)
> See also 68:44

Dreadful Imr امر See Grievous

Dream Ruya رؤيا See Vision

Drugget Abquary عبقري

> Reclining upon green cushions and lovely druggets (55:76)

Drunken Sukara سكارى

> Draw not near to prayer when you are drunken untill you know what you are saying (4:43)
> Yet they are not drunk but God's chastisement is terrible (22:2)
> See also 43:46, 22:2

Dry clay Salsal صلصال

> We created men of a clay of mud moulded (15:26)
> He created man of a clay like the potter's (55:14)
> See also 15:28, 33

Dry date stalk Urjun عرجون

> Till it returns like an aged palm-bough (36:75)

Dry Land Barr بر

> He knows what is in land and see (6:59)
> It is He who conveys you on the land (10:22)
> He will not cause the shore to swallow you up (17:68)
> See also 5:96, 6:63, 97, 17:67, 70, 27:63, 29:65, 30:41, 31:32

Dust Ghabarah غبرة

> Some faces on that day shall be dusty (80:40)

E

Earn Kasaba كسب

> Spend of the good things you have earned (2:267)
> There awaits them that they have earned (2:134)
> God may recompense every soul for its earnings (14:134)
> See also 2:79, 81, 134, 141, 202, 225, 264, 281,286, 3:25, 155, 4:88,111, 112, 5:38, 6:3, 70,120, 129, 158, 164,7:39, 96, 9:82, 10:8, 27, 52, 13:33, 34, 14:18, 15:84,18:58, 30:41, 31:34, 35:45, 36:65, 39:24,48, 50,51,40:17, 82, 41:17, 42:22, 30, 54, 45:10, 14, 22, 52:21, 74:38, 83:14, 111:12

Earth Ard أرض

> Do not corrupt the earth (2:11)
> It is He who created for you all that is in the earth (2:29)
> Surely to God belongs the kingdom of the heavens and of the earth (9:116)
> See also 2:22,27, 30, 36, 60, 61, 71, 107,116, 117, 164, 168, 205, 251, 255, 267, 273, 284, 3:5, 29, 83, 91, 109, 129,133,137,156, 180 189, 190, 191, 4:42, 97, 100,101, 126, 131, 132, 170, 171, 5:17, 18, 21, 26, 31,32,33, 36,40,64,97,106,120, 6:1, 3, 6, 11, 12, 4, 35, 38, 59, 71, 73, 75, 79, 101, 116, 165, 7:10, 24, 54, 56, 73, 74, 85, 96, 100, 127, 128, 129, 137, 146, 158, 168, 176, 185, 187, 8:26, 63, 67, 73, 9:2, 25, 36, 38, 74, 118, 10:36, 14, 18, 23, 24, 31, 54, 55, 61, 66, 68, 73, 83, 99, 101, 11:6, 7, 20, 44, 61, 64, 85, 107, 108, 116, 123,12:9,21,55, 56, 73, 80, 101, 105, 109, 13:3, 4, 15, 16, 17, 18, 25, 31, 33, 41, 14:2, 8, 10, 13, 14, 19, 26, 32, 38, 48, 15:19, 39, 85, 16:3, 13, 15, 36, 45, 49, 52, 65, 73, 77, 17:4, 37, 44, 55, 76, 90, 95,

99, 102, 103, 104, 18:7, 14, 26, 45, 47, 51, 84, 94, 19:40,
65, 90, 93, 20:4, 6, 53, 57, 63, 21:4, 16, 19, 21, 30, 31, 44,
56, 71, 81, 105, 22:5, 18, 41, 48, 63, 64, 65, 70, 23:18, 71,
79, 84. 112, 24:35, 41, 42, 55, 57, 64, 25:2, 6, 59, 63,
26:7, 24, 35, 152, 27:25, 48, 60, 61, 62, 64, 65, 69, 75, 82,
87, 28:4, 56, 19, 39,57, 77, 81, 83, 29:20, 22, 36, 39, 40,
44, 52, 56, 61, 63, 30:3, 8, 9, 18, 19, 22, 24, 25, 26, 27,
42, 50, 31:10, 16,18, 20,25, 26,27, 34, 32:4, 5, 10, 27,
33:27, 72, 34:12, 3,9,14, 22,24, 35:1,3 9, 38, 39, 40, 41,
44, 36:33, 36, 37:5, 38:10, 26, 27, 28, 66, 39:5,10, 21, 38,
44, 46, 47, 63, 67, 68, 69, 74, 40:21, 26, 29, 57, 64, 65,
82, 41:9, 11, 15, 39, 42:4,5, 11, 12, 27, 29, 31, 42, 49, 53,
43:9, 10, 60, 82,84, 85, 45:3, 5, 13, 22, 27, 36, 37, 46:3, 4,
20, 32, 33, 47:10, 22, 48:4, 7, 14, 16, 18, 50:4, 7, 38, 44,
51:20, 23, 48, 53:31, 32, 54:12, 55:10, 29, 56:14, 57:1, 2,
4, 5, 10, 17, 21, 22, 58:60, 59:1, 24, 61:1, 62:1,10, 63:7,
64:1, 3, 4, 65:12, 67:15, 16, 24, 69:14, 70:14, 71:17, 19,
26, 72:10, 12, 73:14, 20, 77:25, 78:6, 37, 79:30, 80:26,
84:13, 85:9, 86:12, 88:20,89:21, 91:6,99:1,2

Earthen vase Fakhkhar فخار

He created man of clay like the potter's (55:14)

Earthquake Rajfah رجفة

So the earthquake seized them (7:78)
See also 7:91, 155, 29:37

Ease Yassara يسر See Make easy

Eden Adn عدن

Gardens of Eden which they shall enter (13:23)
See also 9:72, 16:31, 18:31, 19:61, 20:76, 35:33, 38:50,
40:8, 61:12, 98:8

Egypt Misr مصر

> O my people, do I not possess the kingdom of Egypt (43:51)
> See also, 2:61, 10:87, 12:21, 99

El-Judi Judi جودي

> And the Ark settled on El-Judi (11:44)

Elias Ilyas الياس See Elijah

Elijah Ilyas الياس

> Righteous 6:85
> Envoy 37:123

Elisha alyasa الياس

> Remember also Our servants, Ishmael, Elisha, and Dhul Kifl (38:48)
> See also, 6:86

Emigrate Hajara هاجر

> Love whosoever emigrated to them (59:9)
> See also 2:218, 3:195, 4:89, 97, 100, 8:72, 74, 75, 9:20, 100, 117, 16:41, 110, 22:58, 33:6, 50, 59:8, 9, 60:10

Encompass Haqa حاق

> They shall be encompassed by that they mocked at (11:8)
> Evil devising encompasses only those who do it (35:43)
> See also 6:10, 16:34, 21:41, 39:48, 40:45, 83, 45:33, 46:26

Encroach Bagha بغى See Be insolent

End Aqibah, Uqba عاقبة، عقبى

> The end of those that did evil was evil (30:10)

| ENDEAR | 53 | ENEMY |

See also 3:137, 6:11, 135, 7:84, 86, 103, 128, 10:39, 83, 11:49, 12:109, 16:36, 20:132, 22:41, 287:14, 51,69, 28:37, 40, 83, 30:9, 10, 42, 31:22, 35:44, 37:73, 40:21,82, 43:25, 47:10, 59:17, 65:9

For Uqba 13:22, 24, 35, 42, 91:15

Endear Habbaba حبب

God has endeared to you belief (49:7)

Endear vt Habbaba حبب

God has endeared to you belief (49:7)

Endow vt Razaqa رزق See Provide

Endure patiently Sabara صبر

Peace be upon you, for that you were patient (13:24)

Moses, we will not endure one sort of food (2:61)

See also 2:45, 61, 153, 155, 175, 177, 249, 250, 3:17, 120, 142, 125, 146, 186, 4:25, 6:34, 7:87, 126, 128, 137, 8:46, 65, 66, 11:11, 49, 115, 12:18, 83, 13:22, 24, 14:12, 21, 16:42, 96, 110, 126, 127, 18:28, 67, 69, 72, 75, 78, 82, 20:130, 21:85, 22:35, 23:111, 25:20, 42, 75, 20:54, 80, 30:60, 32:24, 33:35, 37:102, 38:6, 17, 44, 39:10, 40:55, 77, 41:35, 42:43, 46:35, 49:5, 50:39, 52:16, 48, 70:5, 76:12, 90:17, 103:3

Enduring Baqi باقي

World to come is better and more enduring (87:17)

God is better and more enduring (20:73)

He made it a word enduring (43:28)

See also 16:96, 18:46, 19:76, 20:71, 127, 131, 26:120, 28:60, 37:77, 42:36, 69:8

Enemy 'Aduw عدو

God is an enemy to the unbelievers (2:98)
Satan is for you a manifest foe (7:22)
We have appointed to every prophet an enemy (25:31)
See also 2:36, 97, 98, 168, 208, 3:103, 4:45, 92, 101, 6:112, 142, 7:24, 129, 150, 8:60, 9:83, 114, 120, 12:5, 17:53, 18:50, 20:39, 80, 117, 123,25:31, 26:77, 28:8 15, 19, 35:6, 36:60, 41:19,29, 28, 43:62, 67, 46:6, 60:1,2, 61:14, 63:4, 64:14

Enmity 'Udwan عدوان

Do not help each other to sin and enmity (5:2)
Conspire not together in sin and enmity (58:9)
See also : 2:85, 193, 4:30, 5:62, 28:28, 58:8

Enmity 'Adawah عداوة

We have stirred up among them enmity (5:14)
Satan only desires to precipitate enmity and hatred (5:91)
See also 5:64,82,41:34, 60:4

Enmity Ghill غل See Rancour

Enoch Idris ادريس See Idris

Ensample Imam امام See Leader

Enter Dakhala دخل

Enter it not until leave is given (24:28)
There is no fault in you that you enter houses uninhabited (24:29)
Did you suppose you should enter Paradise (2:214)
Enter Paradise for that you were doing (61:32)
See also 2:58,111,114, 208, 214, 3:37,97,142,4:23, 124, 154,5:21, 22,23, 24, 61,7:38, 40, 46, 49, 161, 12:36, 58, 67, 68, 69, 88,99,13:23 (2) 15:46, 52, 16:29, 31,31,17:7,

18:35, 39, 19:60, 24:27, 28,29,61, 27:18,34,44,28:15, 33:14, 53, 35:33, 36:26, 38:22, 39:72, 73, 40:40, 60, 76, 43:70, 48:27, 49, 14, 50:34, 51:25, 66:10, 68:24, 71:28, 89:29, 30, 110:2

Equal كفؤ

And equal to Him not any one (112:4)

Equipment Uddah عدة See Counterpoise

Err Dalla ضل See Go astray

Err vt Ghawa غوى

Adam disobeyed his Lord, and so he erred (20:121)
See also 2:256, 7:146, 175, 202, 15:42, 19:59, 26:91, 94, 224, 28:63, 37:32, 53:2

Er-Rakeem Raqim الرقيم

Ad, and Thamood, and the men of the Cave and Er-Rakeem were among Our signs a wonder? (18:9)

Er-Rass Rass الرس

Ad, Thamood and the men of Er-Rass (25:36)
See also, 50:12

Essence Umm أم

Eternal Qayyum قيوم See Everlasting

Eternity Khuld خلد

Is that better or the Garden of Eternity? (25:15)
See also, 10:52, 20:120, 21:34, 32:14, 41:28

Even Safsaf صفصف See Level

Evening Asil أصيل

They are recited to him at the dawn and in the evening (25:5)

And remember the Name of thy Lord at the dawn and in the evening (76:25)

See also 7:205, 13:15, 24:36, 33:42, 48:9

Eventide Asil أصيل See Evening

Everlasting Qayyum قيوم

God there is no God but He the living, The Everlasting (2:255)

See also, 3:2, 20:111

Ever-Sure Matin متين See Sure

Evidence Bayyinah بينة

Moses came to you with the clear signs (2:92)

See also 2:87, 99, 159, 185, 209, 211, 213, 253, 3:86, 97, 105, 183, 184, 4:153, 5:32, 110, 6:57, 157, 7:73, 85, 101, 105, 8:42, 9:70, 10:13, 15, 74, 11:17, 28, 53, 63, 88, 14:9, 16:44, 17:101, 18:15, 19:73, 20:72, 133, 22:16, 72, 24:1, 28:36, 29:35, 39, 30:9, 47, 34:43, 354:25, 40, 40:22, 28, 34,50, 66, 83, 43:63, 45:17, 25, 46:14, 57:9, 25, 50:5, 61:6, 64:6, 98:1, 4

Evil Sayyi'ah سيئة

The recompense of an evil deed shall be the like of it (10:27)

What ever evil visits thee is of thy self (4:79)

Who so earns evil, and is encompassed by his transgression (2:81)

See also 2:271, 3:120, 193, 195, 4:18, 31, 78, 79, 5:12, 65, 6:160, 7:95, 131, 168, 8:29, 10:27, 11:10, 78, 114, 13:6, 22, 16:34, 45, 23:96, 25:70 27:46, 90, 28:54, 84,

29:4, 7, 30:36, 35:10, 39:48, 51, 40:9, 40, 41:34, 42:25, 40, 48, 45:21, 33, 46:16, 47:12, 48:5, 64:9, 65:5, 66:8

Evil suggestions of the Devil Hamazat همزات

I take refuge in thee from the evil suggestions of the satan (23:97)

Exalt A'a'zza أعز

Thou exaltest whom thou wilt (3:26)

Exalted Taala تعالى

God is high exalted above that they associate (7:190)
See also, 6:100, 10:18, 16:1, 17:43, 20:114, 23:93, 116, 27,63, 28:68, 30:40, 39:67, 72:3

Example Imam امام See Leader

Example Mathal مثل See Similitude

Exceed against Farata فرط

Truly we fear he may exceed against us (20:45)

Excel in patience Sabara صابر

O believers, be patient, and excel in patience (3:200)

Exchange vt Baddala بدل See Substitute

Expand Basata بسط See Stretch out

Expend vt Anfaqa أنفق

O Believers, expend of that with which We have provided you (2:254)
The likeness of that they expend in this present life (3:117)
See also 2:3, 195, 215, 219, 254, 261, 262, 64, 265, 267, 270, 272, 273, 274, 3:17, 92, 117, 134, 4:34, 38, 39, 5:64, 8:3, 36, 60, 63, 9:34, 54, 91, 92, 98,

99, 121, 13:22, 14, 31, 16:75, 17:100, 18:42, 22:35, 25:67, 28:54, 32:16, 34:39, 35:29, 36:47, 42:38, 47:38, 57:7, 10, 60:10, 11, 63:7, 10, 64:16, 65:67

Experience Daqa ذاق See Taste

Expiation Kaffarah كفارة

> Whosoever forgoes it as a freewill offering, that shall be for him an expiation (5:45)
> See also 5:89,95

Exquisite wine Rahiq Makhtum رحيق مختوم

> As they are given to drink of a wine sealed (83:25)

Extol Sabbaha سبح See Praise

Extra Nafilah نافلة See Superfluity

Eye 'Ayn عين

> They have eyes but perceive not with them (7:179)
> Thou art before Our eyes (52:48)
> We would have obliterated their eyes (36:66)
> See also 3:13, 5:45, 83, 7:116, 195, 8:44, 9:91, 11:31, 37, 12:84, 15:88, 18:28, 101, 19:26, 20:39, 40, 131, 21:61, 23:27, 25:74, 28:9, 13, 32:17, 33:19, 51, 40:19, 43:71, 54:14, 37, 90:8, 102:7

Eye Basar بصر

> Their eyes and their skins bear witness against them (41:20)
> God has set a seal on ..... their eyes (16:108)
> He appointed for you hearing, and sight (32:9)
> See also 2:7,20, 3:13, 6:46, 103,110, 7:47,10:31, 14:41, 15:15, 16:77, 78,17:36, 21:97, 22:46, 23:78, 24:30, 31, 37, 43, 44, 33:10, 38:45, 63, 41:22, 45:23, 46:26, 47:23,

50:22, 53:17, 54:7, 50, 59:2, 67:3, 4, 23, 68:43, 51, 70:44, 75:7, 79:9

Eye-sight Basar بصر See Eye

Ezra Uzayr عزير

Ezra is the son of God (9:30)

F

Face Adhqan أذقان See Chin

Faciliate Yassar يَسَّرَ See Make easy

Faith Iman إيمان

    Rejecters of 2:6-7, 165-167, 3:4,10, 12, 21-22, 90-91, 116, 181-184, 4:136, 137, 167-168
    Signs of 2:165, 285
    Sellers of 3:77, 177
    Strengthened in danger and disaster 3:173
    And Righteousness, 5:69
    Ransom not accepted 5:36-37
    Follow ancestral ways 5:104
    Destroyed 6:6
    Ask for angel to be sent down 6:8-9
    Lie against their own souls 6:24
    Will see Truth in Hereafter 6:28-30
    Will be in confusion 6:110
    Hearts inclined to deceit 6:113
    Followed by unbelief 16:106-109
    Seven jewels of 23:9
    And charity 57:7-11
    Taste evil result of conduct 64:5-6
    Their way and worship repudiated 109:1-6

Faithful Amin أمين

    I am your adviser, sincere, faithful (7:68)
    See also 12:54, 26:107, 125, 143,162, 178,193, 27:39, 28:26, 44:18, 51, 81:21, 95:3

Fall in ruin Inhara إنهار See Tumble

False Batil باطل See Falsehood

Falsehood Batil باطل

> God blots out falsehood and verifies the truth (42:24)
> We hurt the truth against falsehood and it prevails over it (21:18)
> See also 2:42, 188, 3:71, 191, 4:29, 161, 7:139,8:8,9:34, 11:16,13:17, 16:72, 17:81, 18:56, 22:62, 29:52, 67, 31:30, 34:49, 38:27, 40:5, 41:42, 47:3

Family Bayt بيت See House

Famine Masghabah مسغبة See Hunger

Father Ab أب

> We will serve thy God and the God of thy fathers (2:133)
> Do not marry women that your fathers married (4:22)
> Return you all to your father (12:81)
> Father, why worshippest thou that which neither hears nor sees (19:42)
> See also 2:170, 200, 4:11, 5:104,6:74,87,91,148, 7:27, 28, 70,71,95, 173, 9:23, 24, 114,10:78, 11:62, 87, 109, 12:4, 6,8, 9, 11, 16, 17,38, 40,59,61, 63, 65, 68, 78, 80, 83, 94, 97, 99, 100, 13:23, 14:10, 16:35, 18:5, 80, 82, 19:28, 43, 44, 45, 21:44, 52, 53, 54, 22:78, 23:24, 68, 83, 24:31, 61, 25:18, 26:26, 70, 74, 76, 86, 27:67, 68, 28:23, 25, 26, 36, 31:21, 33:5,40,55,34:43, 36:6, 37:17, 69, 85, 102, 126, 40:18, 43:22, 232,24, 26, 29, 44:8, 36, 45:25, 53:23, 56:48, 58:22, 60:4, 80:35

Fatigue Laza لظى

> Nay, verily it is a furnace (70:15)

Fault Danb ذنب See Sin

Fault Junah جناح

> It is no fault in you, that should seek bounty (2:198)
> See also 2:158, 229, 230, 233, 234, 235, 236, 240, 282
> 4:23, 24, 101, 102, 128, 5:93, 24:29, 58, 60, 61, 33:5, 51, 55, 60:10

Favour Faddal فضل See Prefer

Fear Ba's بأس See Might

Fear Khashiya خشى

> So fear not men (5:44)
> Performs the prayer, and pays the alms and fear none but God alone (9:18)
> The provision is for those of you who fear sin (4:25)
> See also 2:150, 3:173, 4:9, 25, 77, 5:3, 44:52, 9:13, 18, 13:21, 17:31, 100, 18:80, 20:3, 44, 77, 94, 21:28, 49, 23:57, 24:52, 31:33, 33:37, 39, 35:18, 28, 36:11, 39:23 50:33, 59:21, 67:12, 79:19, 26, 45, 80:9, 87:10, 98:8

Fear of God Khashiyatullah خشية الله

> Its reality 2:2, 98:8
> As He should be feared 3:102
> Command to people of the Book and Muslims 4:131
> Piety and restraint 47:17
> Unseen 67:12
> Of His displeasure 70:27
> Righteousness 74:56

Fear vt Ittaqa إتقى

> But piety is to be god-fearing (2:103)
> Fear you God, and know that God is with the god-fearing (2:194)

See also 2:21, 24, 41, 48, 63, 66, 103, 123, 177, 179, 180, 189, 187, 197, 203, 206, 212, 223, 224, 231, 233, 241, 278, 281, 282, 283, 3:15, 50, 28, 76, 115, 102, 120, 123, 125, 130, 133, 179, 198, 200, 4:1, 9, 77, 128, 129, 131, 5:2, 4, 7, 8, 11, 25, 35, 46, 57, 65, 88, 93, 96, 100, 108, 12, 6:32, 5:69, 153, 155, 7:35, 15:45, 69, 16:2, 30, 31, 52, 128, 19:79, 85, 20, 47, 113, 21:48, 22:1, 23:23, 32, 52, 87, 24, 34, 52, 25:15, 74, 26:11, 106, 108, 90, 110, 124, 126, 142, 131, 132, 144, 150, 161, 163, 177, 179, 184, 27:53, 28:83, 29:16, 30:31, 31:1, 32, 37, 55, 70, 36:45, 30:28, 49, 10, 16, 20, 24, 28, 33, 61, 57, 73, 41, 18, 43:35, 63, 67, 47, 44:51, 45:19, 49:1, 10, 12, 50:31, 51:17, 57:28, 58:9, 59:7, 18, 60:11, 65:4, 5, 60:34, 69:48, 71:3, 73:17, 78:31, 92:5

Female Untha أنثى

The male is not as the female (3:36)

God know what every female bears (13:8)

O mankind, We have created you male and female (49:13)

See also 2:178, 3:36, 195, 4:11, 117, 124, 176, 6:143, 144, 16:58, 97, 17:40, 35:150, 40:40, 41:47, 42:49, 50, 43:19, 53:21, 27, 45, 75:39, 92:13

Fetter Ghalla غل See Defraud

Fetters Aghlal أغلال

We put fetters on the necks of the unbelivers (34:33)

We have prepared for the unbelievers chains (76:4)

See also 7:157, 13:5, 36:8, 40:71

Fiction Hizb حزب See Party

Fierce Asib عسيب

> This is a fierce day (11:77)

Fight for the faith Jahada جاهد See Struggle

Fighting Jihad جهاد

> In the cause of God 2:190-193, 4:84
> Prescribed 2:216, 2:224
> In the prohibited month 2:217
> By Children of Israel 2: 246-251
> In the cause of God and oppressed men and women 4:74-76
> Till no more 8:39
> Against odds 8:65
> In case of 9:5-6, 12, 13-16
> Those who believe not, and reject Truth 9:29
> With firmness 9:123
> Permitted to those who are wronged 22:39-41
> When, and till when 47:4
> And the faint-hearted 47:20
> Exemptions from 48:17

Filth Ghislin غسلين See Foul pus

Final end Muntaha منتهى

> This is naught but the fairy tales of the ancient ones (6:25) See also 8:31, 16:24, 23:83, 25:5, 27:68, 46:17, 68:15, 83:13

Find fault lamaza لَمَزَ

> Find not fault with one another (49:11)
> See also 9:58, 79

Finery Zinah زينة See Adornment

Fire Nar نار

> Fear the fire, whose fuel is men and stones (2:24)
> Taste the chastisement of the fire (32:20)
> See also 2:17, 39, 80, 81, 126, 167, 174, 175, 201, 217, 221, 257, 266, 275, 3:10, 16, 24, 103, 116, 131, 151, 183, 185, 191, 192, 4:10, 14, 30, 56, 145, 5:29, 37, 64, 72, 6:27, 128, 7:12, 36, 38, 44, 47, 50, 8:14, 9:17,35, 63, 68, 81, 109, 10:8, 27, 11:16, 17, 98, 106, 113, 13:5, 17, 35, 14:30, 50 15:27, 16:62, 18:29,53, 96, 20:10, 21:39, 69, 22:19, 72, 23:104, 24:35, 57, 27:7, 7, 8, 90, 28:29, 41, 29:24, 25, 32:20, 33:667, 34:42, 35:32, 36:80, 38:27, 59, 61, 64, 76, 39:8, 16, 19, 40:6, 41, 43, 46, 47, 49, 72, 41:19, 24, 28, 40, 45:54, 46:20, 34, 47:12, 15, 51:13, 52:13, 14, 54:48, 55:15, 35, 56:71, 57:15, 58:17, 59:3m 64:10, 66:6, 10, 71:25, 72:23, 74:31, 85:15, 87:12, 88:4, 90:20, 92:14, 98:6, 101:11, 104:6, 111:3

Fire Sa'ir سعير See Blaze

Fissure Futur فطور

> Return thy glaze; seest thou any fissure? (67:3)

Flame laza لظى See Furnace

Flame Shihab شهاب

> And he is pursued by a manifest flame (15:18)
> See also 27:7, 37:10, 72:8,9

Flaunt Tabarraja تبرج See Display

Flaw Futur فطور See Fissure

Flocks Na 'am نعام See Cattle

Fodder Abb أبّ See Pastures

Foe ʿAduw عدو See Enemy

Folk Unas أناس See People

Footstep Athar أثر

>And we sent, following in their footsteps, Jesus son of Mary (5:46)
>See also 18:6, 64, 20:84,96, 30:50, 36:123, 37:L70, 40:21, 82, 43:22, 23, 48:29, 57:27

Forbid Naha نهى

>Whatever he forbids you, give over (59:7)
>Perform the prayer, and bid unto honour and forbid dishonour (31:17)
>See also 3:104, 110, 114, 4:31, 161, 5:63, 6:26, 28, 7:20, 22, 157, 165, 166, 9:67, 71, 112, 11:62, 88, 116, 15:70, 16:90, 22:41, 29:45, 40:66, 59:7, 60:8, 9, 79:40, 96:9

Forbid vt, Hassama حسّم

>God has permitted trafficking, and forbidden usury (2:275)
>See also 2:173, 3:93, 4:160, 5:72, 6:119, 140, 143, 144, 146, 148, 150, 15, 17:32, 33, 50, 9:29, 37, 16:35, 115, 118, 17:33, 25:68, 27:91, 28:12

Forbidden Haram حرام See Holy

Forceful Dhu mirrah ذو مرّة See Very strong

Foreign tongue Ajamiy عجمى See Non-Arab

Forge Iftara إفترى

>Whosoever associates with God any thing, has indeed forged a mighty sin (4:48)

Who does greater evil than he who forges against God a lie? (6:93)

So leave them to their forging (6:137)

See also 3:24, 94, 4:48, 50, 5:103, 6:21, 24 93, 112, 137, 138, 140, 144, 7:37, 53, 89, 152, 10:17, 30,37, 38,59, 60, 69, 11:13, 18, 21, 35,50, 12:111, 16:56, 87, 101, 105, 116, 17:73, 18:15, 20:61, 21:5, 23:38, 25:4, 28:36,75, 29:68, 32:3, 34:8,43, 42:24, 46:8, 28, 60:12,61:7

Forgive Ghafara غفر

You do not wish that God should forgive you (24:22)

Surely God forgives sins altogether (39:53)

He will forgive who He will and chastise whom He will (2:284)

See also 2:58, 286, 3:16, 31, 129, 135, 4:48, 116, 137, 168, 5:18, 40, 118, 7:23, 149, 151, 155, 161, 169, 8:29, 38,70, 9:80, 1:47, 12:92, 14:10,41, 20:73, 23:109, 118, 24:22, 26:51, 82, 86, 28:16, 33:71, 38:35, 40:37, 42:37, 45:15,46:31, 47:34, 48:2, 14,57:28, 59:10, 60:5, 61:12, 63:6, 64:14, 17, 66:8,71:47, 28

Forgive vt Afa عفا See Remit

Forgiveness Ghufran غفران

Our Lord, grant us thy forgiveness (53:32)

See also 2:175, 221, 263, 268, 3:133, 136,157, 4:96, 5:9,8:4,74,11:11,13:6,22:50,24:26, 33:35, 34:4, 35:7, 36:11,41:43,47:15,48:29,49:3,57:20,21,67:12,74:56

Forgiveness Khashiyah خشية

Forgiveness 2:109, 4:48, 110, 116, 7:199, 39:53, 42:5, 45:14, 53:32, 57:21

Forgiveness, by Believer, for people of the Book 2:109

Words for 2:109
Hold to, and cmmand the right 7:199
By God, for sins other than joining gods with God 4:48, 110, 116
God forgives all sins 39:53
Duty of believers 42:37, 40, 45:14
Angels pray for forgiveness of all beings on earth 42:5
Forgive, even when angry 42:37
And reconciliation 42:40
Believers to forgive those who do not look forward to the days of God 45:14
God forgives those who avoid great sins and shameful deeds 53:32
Be foremost in seeking 57:21

Forgiver Ghffar غفار See All-forgiving

Former condition Hafirah حافرة

Are we being restored as we were before?(79:10)

Fornicate Zana زنا

Nor slay the soul God has bidden except by right, neither fornicate (25:68)

The fornicatress—none shall marry her but a fornicator (24:3)

See also 24:2, 3, 17:32, 60:12

Forsake vt Wadhara وزر See Leave

Fortress Husun حصون

They thought that their fortresses would defend them (59:2)

Foul pus Ghislin, Ghassaq غسلين، غساق

Neither any food gave foul pus (69:36)

For Ghassaq 38:57, 78:25

Fount of Abundance Kawthar كوثر

    Surely we have given thee abundance (108:1)

Fragment Idin عضين

    Who have broken the Koran in fragments (15:91)

Fragment, Kisf كسف

    Or till thou makest heaven to fall as thou assertest, on us in fragments (17:92)
    See also 26:187, 30:48, 34:9, 52:44

Fraud Ifk إفك See Slander

Freewill offering Sadaqah صدقة

    The freewill offerings are for the poor and needy (9:60)
    See also 2:196, 263, 264, 271, 276, 4:114, 9:58, 79, 103, 104, 58:12, 13

Fretful Halu هلوع

    Surely man was created fretful (70:19)

Friend Khalil خليل

    Friends in that day shall be foes to one another (43:67)
    See also 4:125, 17:73, 25:28

Frowning Abus عبوس

    We fear from our Lord, a frowning day (76:10)

Frustrate Kabata كبت

    Those who oppose God and His Messenger shall be frustrated (58:5)
    See also 3:127, 58:5

Fuel Hasab حصب

You and that you were serving apart from God, are fuel for Ghenna (21:98)

Fuel Hasab, Hatab حصب، حطب

You and that you were serving apart from God, are fuel for Gehenna (21:98)
For Hatab 72:15, 114:4

G

Gabriel Jibril جبرئيل

    An enemy to God and His angels and His Messengers, and Gabriel (2:98)
    See also 2:97, 66:4

Gain as booty Ghanimah غنيمة

    Whatever booty you take, the fifth of it is God's (8:41)
    See also 8:69

Gap Farj فرج See Opening

Garden Jannah جَنَّة See Paradise

Garment libas لباس

    We have sent down on you a garment to cover your shameful parts (7:26)
    And We appointed night for a garment (78:10)
    See also 2:187, 7:27, 16:112, 22:23, 25:47, 35, 33

Gather Hashara حشر See Muster

Gather vt. Hashara حشر See Muster

Gentle Wind Rukha رخاء See Soft wind

Gift 'Ata' عطاء

    Thy Lord's gift is not confined (17:20)
    From thy Lord, a gift, a reckoning (78:36)
    See also 11:108, 17:21, 38:39

Gift Hadiyah هدية See Present

Gift Hady هدى See Offering

Give alms Tasaddaqa تَصَدَّقَ See Give freewill offering

Give credence Sadqa صدق See Confirm

Give ear vt Adhina أَذِنَ See Give leave

Give freewill offering Tasaddaqa تَصَدَّقَ

> That you should give freewill offerings is better for you (2:280)
> Whosoever forgoes it as a freewill offering, that shall be for him an expiation (5:45)
> See also 4:92, 9:75, 12:88, 33:35, 57:18, 63:10

Give leave vt Adhina أَذِنَ

> Save for him to whom He gives leave (34:23)
> That God gives leave to whomsoever He wills (53:26)
> Enter it not until leave is given to you (24:28)
> See also 2:97, 102, 213, 221, 49,251,255,279,3:49, 145, 152, 166, 4:25, 64, 5:16, 110, 7:58, 123, 8:66, 9:43, 49, 90, 10:3, 59, 100, 11:105, 12:80, 13:38, 14:1, 11, 23, 25, 16:84,20:71, 109, 22:65, 24:62, 26:49, 33:46, 53, 34:12, 22, 35:32, 40:78, 42:21, 51, 53: 26, 58:10. 59:5, 64:11, 77:36, 78:38, 84:2, 5, 97:4

Give life Ahya أحي

> Whoso gives life to a soul (5:32)
> God gives life and He makes to die (30:156)
> And He revives the earth after it is dead (30:24)
> See also 2:28,73, 164, 243, 258, 259, 260, 3:49, 5:32,6:122,7:158,8:24, 9:116, 10:56, 15:23, 16:65, 97, 22:6,66, 23:80, 25:49, 26:81, 29:63, 30:19, 24, 40, 50, 36:12, 35, 78, 79, 40:11, 68, 41:39, 42:9, 44:8, 45:5, 26, 46:33, 50:11, 43, 53:44, 57:2, 17, 75:40

Give refuge Awa أوى

But He gave you refuge, and confirmed you (8:26)
His kin who sheltered him (70:13)
See also 8:72, 74, 12:69, 99, 23:50, 93:6, 33:51,

Give speech Antaqa أَنْطَقَ

God gave us speech, as He gave every thing (speech) (41:21)
See also 41:21

Give thanks Shakara شَكَرَ See Thank

Give up Wadara وَزَرَ See Leave

Give vt Ata أعطى

Take forcefully what We have given you (2:63)
We gave them a mighty kingdom (4:54)
He gives the wisdom to whomsoever He will (2:269)
See also 2:43, 53, 63, 83, 87, 93, 101:10, 121, 136, 144, 145, 146, 177, 200, 201, 211, 213, 229, 233, 247, 251, 253, 258, 265, 269, 277, 3:19, 20, 23, 73, 79, 81, 84, 148, 170, 180, 186, 187, 194, 4:19, 20, 24, 25, 33, 37, 40, 44,47, 51, 53, 54, 67, 74, 77, 114, 127, 131, 146, 152, 162, 153, 162,163,, 5:5, 12, 20:41, 46, 48, 54, 55, 57, 6:20, 44, 83, 89, 114, 124, 141 154, 165, 7:38, 144, 156 171, 175, 189, 190, 8:70, 9:5, 11, 18, 29, 59, 71, 75, 76, 10:88, 11:13, 28, 31, 63, 110, 12:22,31, 66,101, 13:36, 14:25, 34, 15:81, 87, 16:27, 55, 90, 122, 17:2, 26, 27, 55, 59, 71, 85, 101, 107, 18:10, 33, 40, 62, 65, 84, 96, 19:12, 30, 77, 20:36, 99, 21:48, 51, 73, 74, 79, 84, 22:41, 54, 78, 23:49, 60, 24, 22, 33, 37, 56, 25:35, 27:3, 15, 16, 23, 36, 42, 28:14, 43, 48, 52, 54, 60, 76, 77, 78, 79, 80, 39:27, 47, 49, 66, 30:34, 38, 39, 56, 31:4, 12, 32:13, 23, 33:14, 31,

33, 50, 51, 68, 34:6, 10, 44, 45, 35:40, 37:111, 38:20, 39:49, 40:55, 31:7, 45, 42:20, 36, 43:21, 44:33, 45:16, 17, 47:16, 17, 36, 48:10, 16, 51:16, 52:18, 57:16, 21, 23, 27, 28, 29, 58:11, 13 59:79, 60:10, 11, 65:6, 7, 69:19, 25, 73:20, 74:31, 52, 84:7, 10, 98:4

Giver Wahhab وهاب See All-giver

Glorify Sabbaha سَبَّحَ See Praise

Glory 'Izzah عزّة

    Glory belongs altogether to God (10:65)
    Vain glory seizes him in his sin (2:206)
    The unbelievers glory in their schism (38:2)
    See also 4:139, 26:44, 36:10, 37:180, 38:2, 82, 63:8

Glowing Wahhaj وهاج See Blazing

Gnat Baudah بعوضة

    God is not ashamed to strike a similitude even of a gnat (2:26)

Go astray Dalla ضل

    God makes clear to you lest you go astray (4:176)
    Whosoever goes astray, it is only to his own loss (10:108)
    Whosoever associates with God anything, has gone astray into far error (4:116)
    Whosoever exchanges belief for unbelief has surely strayed from the right way (2:108)
    See also 1:7, 2:198, 282, 3:90, 164, 4:44, 116, 136, 167, 176, 5:12, 60, 77, 105, 6:24, 56, 74, 77, 94, 117, 140, 7:37, 53, 60 149, 179, 10:30, 32, 108, 11:21, 12:8, 30, 95, 13:14, 14:3, 18, 15:56, 16:87, 126, 17:15, 48, 67, 72, 18:104,

19:38, 20:52, 92, 123, 21:54, 22:12, 23:106, 25:9, 17, 34, 42, 44, 26:20, 86, 96, 27:92, 28:50, 75, 85, 31:11, 32:10, 33:36, 34:8, 24, 50, 36:24, 47, 37:69, 71, 38:26, 39:22, 41, 40,:25, 50, 74, 41:48, 52, 42:18, 43:40, 46:5, 28, 36, 50:27, 53:2, 30, 54:24, 47, 56:51, 92, 60:1, 62:2, 67:29, 68:7, 26, 71:24, 83:32, 93:7

Go in Dakhala دخل See Enter

Go into ruin Fasada فسد See Be corrupted

Go round Tafa طاف

    They shall go round between it and between hot, boiling water (55:44)
    There shall be passed around them platters of gold (43:71)
    See also 2:125,22:26,37:45,52:24,56:17,76:19

Goal Muntaha منتهى See Final end

Goal Wijhah وجهة See Direction

God Allah الله

    Sealed the hearts and sights of the pagans 2:7,7:101
    Mocks at those who mock 2:15
    Encompasses the pagans 2:19, 4:108,
    Makes the dead alive 2:173
    Not ignorant of the deeds 2:74, 85,140,144
    Cursed upon the pagans 2:88, 4:46
    Of great mercy 2:105, 3:74
    Is kind with the people 2:143, 218, 225,3:30
    Powerful 2:148, 220
    Wants to give ease 2:185
    Knows every good deed 2:197
    Hasty in reckoning 2:202
    Does not like ruin 2:205

Gives provision to whom He wants 2:212
Guides whom He wants 2:213
Is wise 2:220, 228
Is ever lasting 2:224, 256
Clarifies the signs 2:242, 266
Is knowledgeable 2:246, 286, 3:29
Is wide 2:247, 261
Is with the patient 2:249
Is the only god, 2:255, 3:2, 3:18, 62
Does not like the pagan 2:276
Is severe in punishment 3:11,8:48
To Him in return 3:28
Obey Him 3:32, 5:92
Does what He wants 3:40
The best deceitful 3:54,8:30
Does not like the wrong-doers 3:57
Is the friend of believers 3:68
Does not guide the wrong-doers 3:86, 3:140
Does not want wrong 3:108
Forgives whom He wants 3:129, 5:40
Punishes whom He wants 3:129, 5:40
Will reward the thank-givers 3:144
Likes the patient 3:46
Likes the good-doers 3:148
Is the best what is hidden in the hearts 3:154
Sent the messenger 3:164
Does not inform about the unseen 3:179
For Him is the kingdom of the heavens and the earth 3:189, 4:170
Wants to forgive 4:27
Ask Him, 4:32
Worship Him 4:36, 10:104
Purifies whom He wants 4:49

Is severe in power 4:84
Will carry to Day of Resurrection 4:87
Preferred the fighter on the wisdom 4:113
Took Abraham a friend 4:125
Will give the believers the reward 4:146
Dislikes the announcement of the evil 4:148
Spoke to Moses 4:164
Is witness 4:166, 6:19
Fear Him 5:8, 112
Took the agreement of the children of Ismail 5:12
Creates what He likes 5:17
Accepts that of the god fearing 5:27
Does not like the destroyers 5:64
Deprived the polytheist from paradise 5:71
Tastes the believers 5:94
Made Ka'ba the sacred house 5:97
Knows every secret and open them 5:99, 16:19
Humiliated whom He wants 6:39
Saves from problems 6:64, 7:89
The order is for Him 7:54
Wants to prove the truth as truth 8:7
Made good news 8:10
Distinguishes bad from good 8:37
Keep patience 8:46
Is enough for the prophet and his followers 8:64
Helped the believers 9:25
Will enrich the believers 9:28
Wants to punish them in this world 9:55
Promises the hypocrites and pagans, the Fire 9:68,85
Loves the pure persons 9:108
Calls to peace 10:25
Did not take any son 10:68,18:4
Is the watcher 11:2, 33:52

Raised the skies without pillars 13:2
Knows what is in the womb of a lady 13:8
Strikes the similitude 13:17, 14:24, 25
Whom He misled is not guided 13:33
Sent down water 16:65
Prefers one over the other in provision 16:71
Made shadow 16:81
Commands to justice 16:90
He is the Lord 18:38
He defends from the believers 22:38
Never deceives 22:47, 39:20
Is the light of the skies and the earth 24:35
Makes day and night 24:44
Created every creature of water 24:45
Is the Lord of the great throne 27:26
He will resurrect 29:30
His remembrance is greater 29:45
Sends the airs 30:48, 35:9
Did not make two hearts for a man 33:4
Is more deserving to be feared 33:37
Created the animal 20:79
Remove the untruth 42:12
Speaks through revelation or behind the veil 42:51
Appointed the sea 45:12
To Him belongs the army of the skies and the earth 48:7
Promises forgiveness to the believers 48:29
Does not like pride 57:23
He has great reward 64:15
Gives every one as per his ability 65:7
Made the earth a bed 71:19

God-fearing Taqiy تقی

God fearing Taqwa تقوى

> The noblest among you in the sight of God is the most god fearing (49:13)
> See also 19:13, 18, 63, 92:17

God fearing Taqwa تقوى

> But the best provision is god-fearing (2:197)
> See also 2:237,5:2, 8,7:26,9:108,20:132,22:32,37,47:17, 48:26, 49:3, 58:9,74:56, 91:8, 96:12

Godly man Rabbani ربّاني

> Be you godly man in that you know the book (3:79)
> See also 5:44,63

Gods Alihah آلهة

> There is no god but He (2:163)
> You have no god other than He (7:65)
> See also 2:255, 3:2, 6,18, 62, 4:87, 5:73, 116, 6:19, 46, 74, 102, 106, 7:59, 73, 85, 127, 138, 140, 158, 9:31, 129, 10:90, 11:14, 50, 53, 54, 61, 84, 101, 13:30, 15:96, 16:2, 51,17:22, 39, 42, 18:14, 15, 19:46, 81, 20:8, 14, 88,97, 98, 21:21, 22, 24, 25, 29, 36, 43, 59, 62, 68, 87, 99, 23:23, 32, 91,116, 117, 25:3, 42, 43, 68, 26:29, 213, 27:26, 60, 61, **62, 63**, 64, 28:38, 70, 71, 72, 88, 35:3, 36:23, 37:35, **36, 86**, 91, 38:5, 6, 65, 39:6, 40:362, 65, 43:45, 58, 44:8, **44:8**, 45:23, 46:22, 28, 47:19, 50:26, 51:51, 52:43, 59:22, 64:13, 71:23, 73:9

Gog Yajuj ياجوج

> When Gog and Magog are unloosed, and they slide down out of every slope (21:98)
> See also 18:94

Goliath Jalut جالوت

They routed them, by the leave of God, and David slew Goliath (2:251)
See also 2:249,250

Good deeds Khayrat خيرات

We revealed to them the doing of good deeds (21:73)
See also 2:148, 3:114, 5:48, 9:88, 21:90,23:56, 61, 35:32, 55:70

Good example Uswah أسوة See Model

Good Khayr خير

Whatever good you expend shall be repaid to you in full (2:272)
Let there be one nation of you, calling to good (3:104)
Whosoever has done an atom's weight of good shall see it (99:71)
See also 2:54, 61, 103, 105, 106, 110, 158,180, 184, 197, 215, 216 220, 221, 263, 269, 271, 272, 273, 280, 315, 26, 30, 54, 110, 115, 150, 157, 178, 180, 198, 4:9, 25, 46,59,66, 77, 114, 127, 128, 149, 170, 171, 5:114, 6:17, 32, 57, 158, 7:12, 26, 85, 87, 89, 155, 169, 188, 8:19, 23, 30, 70, 9:3, 41, 61, 74, 109, 10:11, 58, 107, 109, 11:31, 84, 86, 12:39,57, 59, 64, 80, 109, 16:30, 76, 95, 126, 17:11, 35, 18:36, 40, 44, 46, 81, 95, 19:73, 76, 20:73, 131, 21:35, 89, 22:11, 30, 36, 58 77, 23:29, 72, 109, 118, 24:11, 12, 27, 33, 60, 25:10, 15, 24, 27:36, 59, 89, 28:24, 26,60,80, 84, 29:16, 30:38, 33:19, 25, 34:39, 37:62, 38:32, 47, 48, 76, 41:40, 49, 42:36, 43:32, 52, 28, 44:37, 46:11, 47:21, 49:5, 11, 50:25, 54:43,58:12, 61:11, 62:9, 11, 64:16, 66:5, 68:12, 32, 70:21, 41, 73:20, 87:17, 93:4, 97:3, 98:7, 99:7, 100:8

Good pleasure Mardat مرضاة

Those who expend their wealth, seeking God's good pleasure (2:265)

Made lawful to thee, seeking the good pleasure of thy wives (66:1)

See also 2:207, 4:114, 60:1

Good pleasure Ridwan رضوان

Whereby God guides whosoever follows His good pleasure (5:16)

See also 3:15, 62, 174, 9:21, 72, 109, 47:29, 57, 59:8

Good thing Hasanah حسنة

Whosoever gains a good deed, we shall give him increase of good (42:23)

See also 2:201, 3:120, 4:40, 78, 79, 85, 6:160, 7:95, 131, 156, 168, 9:50, 11:114, 13:6, 22, 16:30, 41, 122, 25:70, 27:46, 89, 28:54, 84, 39:10, 41:34

Good Tidings Bushra بشرى

God wrought this not, save as good tiding to you (3:126)

And good tidings to the good-doers (46:12)

No good tidings that day for the sinners (25:22)

See also 2:97, 8:10, 10:64, 11:69, 74, 12:19, 16:89, 102, 27:2, 29:31, 39:17, 57:12

Good works Khayrat خيرات See Good deeds

Goods Mal مال

We will try you with some thing of fear and hunger, and diminution of goods. (2:155)

Wealth and sons are the adornment of the present world (18:46)

See also 2:177, 188, 247, 261, 262, 264, 265, 274, 279, 3:10, 116, 186, 4:2, 5, 6, 10, 24, 29, 34, 38, 95, 161,

5:152, 8:28, 36, 72, 9:20, 24, 34, 41, 44, 55, 69, 81, 85, 88, 103, 111, 10:88, 11:29, 87, 17:6, 34, 64, 18:34, 39, 19:77, 23:55, 24:33, 26:88, 27:36, 30:39, 33:27, 34:35, 37, 47:36, 48:11, 49:15, 51:19, 57:20, 58:17, 59:8, 61:11, 63:9, 64:15, 68:14, 69:28, 70:24, 71:12, 21, 74:12, 89:20, 90:6, 92:11, 18, 104:2, 3, 111:2

Gospel Injil انجيل

And we sent, following, Jesus son of Mary, and gave unto him the Gospel (57:27)
See also 3:3, 48, 65, 5:46, 47, 66, 68, 110, 7:157, 9:11, 48:29

Gourds Yaqtin يقطين

We caused to grow over him a tree of gourds (37:146)

Gracious Hafiy حفى

I will ask my Lord to forgive thee, surely He is ever gracious to me (19:74)
See also 7:187

Grade of honour Darajah درجة See Rank

Grain Habbah حبّة

It is God who splits the grain and the date-stone (6:95)
We may bring forth thereby grain and plants (78:15)
See also 2:261, 6:59, 99, 21:47, 31:16, 36:33, 50:9, 55:12, 80:27

Grapes Inab عنب See Vine

Grass Abb أبّ See Pastures

Great Aziz عزيز See Mighty

Greedy Akkal أكال

Who listen to falsehood, and consume the unlawful (5:42)

Greeks Rum روم

The Greeks have been vanquished (30:2)

Grief Ghamm غم

He sent down upon you, after grief, security (3:154)
We answered him, and delivered him out of grief (21:88)
See also 3:153, 20:40, 22:22

Grievous Asib عسيب See Fierce

Grievous Imr إمر

Thou hast indeed done a grievous thing (18:71)

Grudge Ghill غلّ See Rancour

Gruid Imam إمام See Leader

Guard one self against evil Ittaqa اتقى See Fear

Guardian angels Hafazah حفظة See Recorders

Guardian Hafiz حفيظ

My lord is Guardian over every thing (11:57)
See also 4:80, 6:104, 107, 11:86, 12:55, 34:21, 42:6, 48, 50:4, 32

Guardian Hafiz حافظ

God is the best guardian (12:64)
Over every soul there is a watcher (86:4)
See also 2:255, 4:34, 5:89, 9:112, 12:12, 63, 65, 81, 13:11, 15:9, 17, 21:32, 82, 23:5, 24:30, 31, 33:35, 70:29, 82:10, 83:33, 85:22

Guards of Hell Zabaniyah زَبَانيةٌ

We shall call on guards of Hell (96:18)

Guess work Rajm رجم

>They will say "Five: and their dog was the sixth of them" other guessing at the unseen (18:22)

Guide vt Hada هدى

>We guided them to a straight path (6:87)
>See also 2:143, 185, 198, 213, 3:8, 4:68, 6:71, 84, 87,90,149, 161, 7:30, 43, 9:115, 13:31, 14:12, 21, 16:9,36,121,19:58, 20:50, 79, 122, 22:37, 37:118, 39:18, 57, 41:17, 49:17, 76:3, 87:3, 90:10, 93:7

Guilt Ma'arrah معرة See Crime

Guilty Athim أثيم

>God loves not any ungrateful sinners (2:276)
>See also 4:107, 26:222,44:44, 45:7, 68:12, 83:12

H

Habit Khuluq خلق See Morality

Hallow vt Ahalla أهل

> What has been hallowed to other than God (2:173)
> See also 5:3, 6:145, 16:115

Haman Haman هامان

> Their fate 28:6
> Their sin 28:8
> To build a tower 28:38, 40:36
> Moses to them 29:39, 40:24

Hand maiden Amah أمة See Slave girl

Hardship 'Usr, Ba'sa' عسر، بأساء

> Truly with hardship comes ease (94:5)
> God desires ease for you, and desires not hardship (2:185)
> See also 18:73, 65:7, 94:6
> For Ba'sa' 2:177, 214, 6:42, 7:94

Hardship Darra ضراء See Adversity

Hardship Darra' ضراء

> We seized them with misery and hardship (6:42)
> We let the people taste mercy after hardship has visited them (10:21)
> And endure with fortitude misfortune, hardship and peril (2:177)
> See also 2:214, 3:134, 7:94, 95, 41:50

Harlot Baghiy بغى See Unchaste

Harm Darra ضر See Hurt

Harsh Fazz فظّ

> Hadst thou been harsh and hard of heart (3:159)

Harut Harut هاروت

> Upon Babylon's two angles, Harut and Marut (2:102)

Haste 'Ajal عجل

> Man was created of haste. (21:37)

Hasten Ajjala عجّل

> He has hastened to you (48:20)
> Lord, hasten to us our share (38:16)
> See also 10:11, 17:18, 18:58

Hasten vt. Afrata أفرط

> Theirs shall be the Fire and they are hastened in (16:62)

Hasty Ajul عجول

> Man is ever hasty (17:11)

Hatred Baghda' بغضاء

> Satan only desires to precipitate enmity and hatred (5:91)
> We have stirred up among them enmity and hatred (5:14)
> See also 3:118, 5:64, 60:4

Heap of sand Kathib كثيب

> And the mountains become heap of sand (73:14)

Heart Fua'd فؤاد

> His heart lies not of what he saw (53:11)
> We shall turn about their hearts and their eyes (6:110)
> See also 6:113, 11:120, 14:37,43, 16:78, 17:36, 23:78, 25:32, 28:10, 32:9, 46:26, 53:11, 67:23, 104:7.

Heart Qalb قلب

God has set a seal on their hearts and on their hearing (2:7)

They have hearts but understand not with them (7:179)

See also 2:10, 74, 88, 93, 97, 118, 204, 225, 260 283, 3:7, 8, 103, 126, 151, 154, 156, 159, 167, 4:63, 155, 5:13, 41, 52, 113, 6:25, 43, 46, 7:100, 101, 8:2, 10, 11, 12, 24, 49, 63, 70, 9:8, 15, 45, 60, 64, 77, 87, 93, 110, 117, 125, 127, 10:74, 88, 13:28, 15:12, 16:22, 106, 108, 17:46, 18:14, 28, 57, 21:3, 22:32, 35, 46, 53, 54, 23:60, 63, 24:37, 50, 26:89, 194, 200, 28:10, 30:59, 33:4, 5, 10, 12, 26, 32, 51, 53, 60, 34:23, 27:84, 39:22, 23, 45, 40:18, 35, 41:5, 42:24, 45:23, 47:16, 20, 24, 29, 48:4, 11, 12, 26, 49:3, 7, 14, 50:33, 37, 57:16, 27, 58:22, 59:2, 10, 14, 61:5, 63:3, 64:11, 66:4, 74:31, 79:8, 83:14

Heart Sadr صدر See Breast

Heart vt Rama رمى See Throw

Heavy Asib عسيب See Fierce

Hell Jahannam جهنم See Gehenna

Hell Al-nar النار

Skins roasted and renewed 4:56
Of no profit are hoards and arrogant ways 7:48
For such as took religion to be amusement and were deceived by the life of the world 7:51
Filled with jinns and men 11:119
Drink, boiling fetid water 14:16-17
Death will come, but will not die 14:17
Fetters, liquid pitch faces, covered with Fire 14:49-50
Garment of Fire, boiling water, maces of iron 22:19-22
Blazing fire, furious 25:11-12

Sinners bound together, will plead for destruction, but the destruction will be oft-repeated 25:13-14

Punishment to cover them from above and below 25:55

Fire, wicked forced into it every time they wish to get away 32:20

Men repeatedly warned 36:63

Tree of Zaqqum and boiling water 37:62-67, 44:43-48, 56:52-55

To burn in Hell and taste of boiling fluid and other penalties 38:55-58

Unbelievers led in crowds; previously warned; abode of the arrogant 39:71-72

Dispute and self-recrimination 40:47-50

To dwell for ever punishment not lightened; overwhelming despair 43:74

God not unjust; sinners unjust themselves 43:76

Capacity unlimited 50:30

Sinners known by their marks 55:41

Hell, which they denied; boiling water 55:43-44

Blast of Fire, boiling water, shades of black smoke 56:42-44

Drawing in its breath, bursting with fury 67:25-29

Record in left hand; vain regrets 69:25-29

Seize him bind him, burn him, make him march in a chain 69:30-37

Naught doth it permit to endure, and naught doth it leave alone 74:26-29

Over it are Nineteen 74:30-31

A place of ambush; destination for transgressors; to dwell therein for ages; taste there nothing cool not drink, save boiling fluid, or intensely cold 78:21-25

Day when hell-fire shall be placed in full view 79:35-39

Stain on sinners' hearts; light of God veiled from them; enter the Fire 83:14-16

Faces humiliated enter the Fire; drink boiling water; food bitter Dhari 88:2-7

Brought face to face; will then remember; chastisement and bonds 89:23-26

Bottomless pit; fire blazing fiercely 2:9-11

That which Breaks to pieces; wrath of God 104:4-9

They will neither die nor live 20:74, 87:13

To it are seven Gates 15:44

Is it eternal ? 6:128, 11:107

Who will pass over it ?19:71, 102:6

Helper Adud عضد

> We will strengthen thy arm (28:35)
> See also 18:51

Herm vt Haqa حاق See Encompass

Hew vt Nahata نَحَتَ

> They were hewing the mountains into houses (15:82)
> Do you serve what you hew? (37:95)
> See also 7:74, 26:149

Hide Akhfa أخفى See Conceal

Hide Julud جلود See Skin

Hide Katama كتم See Conceal

Hideous Idd إدّ

> You have indeed advanced something hideous (19:89)

High Aliy علي

> He is the All-high, the All-glorious (2:255)

See also 3:139, 4:34, 9:40, 16:60, 19:50, 57, 20:4, 68,75, 22:62, 30:27, 31:30, 34:23, 37:8, 38:69, 40:12, 42:4, 51, 43:4, 47:35, 53:7, 79:24, 87:1, 92:20

Hill Jabal جبل See Mountain

Hindrance Urdah عرضة

Do not make God a hindrance (2:224)

Holy rite Mansak منسك

We have appointed for every nation a holy rite (22:34)
See also 2:128, 200, 22:67

Holy Haram حرام

Holy Spirit Qudus قدس

The holy spirit sent it down from thy Lord in truth (16:102)
See also 2:87, 253, 5:110

Holy Spirit Ruh روح

The spirit is of the bidding of my Lord (17:85)
See also 2:87, 253, 4:171, 5:110, 15:29, 16:2, 102, 19:17, 21:91, 26:193, 32:9, 38:72, 40:15, 42:52, 58:22, 66:12, 70:4, 78:38, 97:4

Holy things Hurumat حرمات

Holy things demand relation (2:194).
See also 22:30

Honey 'Asal عسل

River, too, of honey purified (46:15)

Honour Izzah عزّة See Glory

Hood Hud هود

Punishment 11:89

Prophet 26:124

Hoopoe Hud-Hud هدهد

How is it with me that I do not see the hoopoe? 27:20

Horizons Afaq آفاق

We shall show them Our signs in the horizons (41:53)
See also 53:7, 81:23

Host Fi'ah فئة

O believers whosoever you encounter stand firm (8:45)
There was no host to help him, apart from God (28:81)
See also 2:249, 3:13, 4:88, 8:16, 19, 45, 48, 18:43

Host Jund جند

To God belongs the hosts of the heavens and the earth (48:7)
We shall assuredly come against them with hosts (27:37)
See also 2:249, 250, 9:26, 40, 10:90, 19:75, 20:78, 26:95, 27:17, 18, 28:6, 8, 39, 33:9, 36:28, 75, 37:173, 38:11, 44:24, 48:47, 51:40, 67:20, 74:31, 85:17

Hour Sa'ah ساعة

To Him is referred the knowledge of the Hour (41:47)
Promise is true and that the Hour there is no doubt of it (18:21)
When their term comes they shall not put it back by a single hour (7:34)
See also 6:31,40, 7:187, 9:117, 10:45, 49, 12:107, 15:85, 16:61, 77, 18:21, 36, 19:75, 20:15, 21:49, 22:17, 25, 25:11, 30:12,14, 55, 31:34, 33:63, 34:3, 30, 40:46, 59, 41:47, 50, 42:17, 18, 43:61, 66,85, 45:27, 32, 46:35, 47:18, 54:1, 46, 79:42

Houris Hur حور

We shall espouse them to wide-eyed houris (44:54)
See also 52:20, 55:72, 56:22

House Bayt بيت

Build for me a house in Paradise (66:11)
Remember that which is recited in your houses (33:34)
It is not piety to come to the houses from the backs of them (2:189)
They destroyed their houses with their own hands (59:2)
In houses (mosques) God has allowed to be raised up (24:36)
See also 2:125, 127, 158, 189, 3:49, 96, 97, 154, 4:15, 100, 5:2, 97, 8:5, 35, 10:87, 11:73, 12:23, 14:37, 15:82, 16:68, 80, 17:93, 22:26, 29, 33, 24:27, 29, 61(9), 26:149, 27:52, 28:12, 29:41(3), 33:13, 33, 53, 43:33, 34, 51:36, 52:4, 65:1, 71:28, 106:3

Humbling Muhin مهين

We have prepared for the unbelievers a humbling chastisement (4:37)
For unbelievers awaits a humbling chastisement (2:90)
See also 3:178, 4:14, 37, 102, 151, 22:57, 31:6, 33:57, 34:14, 44:30, 45:9, 58:5, 16

Humiliation Saghar صغار

Humiliation in God's sight shall befall the sinners (6:124)

Humility Hittah حطة

Enter the gate with humility, and We will forgive you (2:58)
See also 7:161

Hunain Hunain حنين

And on the day of Hunain (9:25)

Hunger Masghabah مسغبة

Or giving food upon a day of hunger (90:14)

Hurt Darra ضرّ

Not the least harm will they do to God (3:176)
He who is astray cannot hurt you (5:105)
They did not hurt any man thereby, save by the leave of God (2:102)
See also 3:111, 120, 144, 177, 4:113, 5:42, 76, 105, 6:17, 71, 7:188, 9:39, 10:12, 18, 49, 107, 108, 11:57, 12:88, 13:18, 16:53, 54, 17:56, 67, 20:89, 21:66, 83, 84, 22:12, 13, 23:75,25:3, 55, 26:73, 30:33, 34:42, 36:23, 39:8, 38, 47:32, 38:11, 58:11, 72:21

Hurt vt Adha أذى

We will surely endure patiently the hurt you may cause Us (14:12)
See also 3:195, 4:16, 7:129, 9:61, 29:10, 33, 57, 58,59, 69

Husband Ba'l بعل See Mate

Hypocrites Munafiqun منافقون

Do not believe in God and the Last Day 2:8
Deceive themselves 2:9
Disease in their hearts 2:10
Make mischief 2:11-12
Fools and mockers 2:13-15
Barter guidance for error 2:16
Deaf, dumb, and blind 2:17-18
In terror and darkness 2:19-20
Dazzling speech; led by arrogance 2:204-206
Refuse to fight 3:167-168
Resort to evil; turn away from Revelation; come when seized by misfortune; to be kept clear of and admonished 4:60-63

Tarry behind in misfortune; wish to share good fortune 4:70-73

Thrown out of the way; reject Faith; renegades; to be seized and slain 4:88-89

Wait for events; think of overreaching God; distracted in mind 4:141-143

In lowest depths of Fire; no helper 4:145

Afraid of being found out 9:64-65

Understanding with each other; perverse; curse of God 9:67-69

Not to be taken as friends 58:14-19

Liars and deceivers, cowards 59:11-14

Liars; screen misdeeds with oaths 63:1-4

I

Iblis Iblis إبليس

> Iblis, what prevented thee to bow thy self before that I created (38: 75)
> See also 2:34, 7:11,15:13,32, 17:61, 18:50, 20:116, 26:95, 34:20, 38: 74, 75

Id Id (a festival) عيد

> Out of heaven that shall be for us a festival (5:114)

Idol Nusub نصب

> As also things sacrificed to idols (5:3)
> See also 5:90, 70:43

Idolate vt Ashraka اشرك See Associate

Idols Awthan أوثان

> You have only taken to yourself idols apart from God (29:25)
> See also 22:30, 29:17

Idols Taghut طاغوت

> Whosoever disbelieves in idols and believes in God (2:256)
> See also 2:257, 4:51, 60, 76, 5:60, 16:36, 39:17

Idris Idris إدريس

> And mention in the Book Idris (19:56)
> See also 21:85

Ignorance Jahalah جهالة

> God shall turn only towards those who do evil in ignorance (94:17)
> See also 6:54, 16:119, 49:6

Illiterate Ummy أمي

>It is He who raised upon from among the common folk a messenger (62:2)
>See also 2:78, 3:20, 75, 7:157, 158

Illiyun Illiyun (probably the name of the highest place in Heaven) عليون

>The book of the pious is in Illiyun (83:18)
>See also 83:19

Illumination Diya' ضياء See Radiance

Impediment Urdahb عرضة See Hindrance

Impose Farada فرض See Appoint

Impudent Ashir أشر

>Nay, rather he is an impudent liar (54:25)
>See also 54:26

Imran Imran عمران

>His family 3:33
>His wife 3:35
>His daughter 66:12

Inclination Hawa هوى See Desire

Increase vt Raba ربا

>What you give in usury, that it may increase upon the people's wealth (30:39)
>See also 13:17, 16, 92, 22:5, 41:39, 69:10

Indecency Fahishah, Fahsha فاحشة، فحشاء

>My Lord has only forbidden indecencies, the inward and the outward (7:33)

See also 3:135, 4:15, 19, 22, 25, 6:151, 7:28, 80, 17:32, 24:19, 27:54, 29:28, 33:30, 42:37, 53:32, 65:1
For Fahisha 2:169, 268, 7:28, 12:24, 16:9o, 24:21, 29:45

Indemnity Diyah دية See Blood wit

Independent Ghaniy غني See Rich

Indulgent Ghafur غفور See All-forgiving

Infirm Har هار See Weak

Injure Bagha' بغى See Be insolent

Injure Darra ضرّ See Hurt

Injustice Hadm هضم

Shall fear neither wrong nor injustice (20:112)

Inner linings Bitanah بطانة See Intimate friend

Innovation Bide بدع

I am not an innovation among the Messengers (46: 9)

Insolence Baghy بغى

We recompensed them for their insolence (6:146)
See also 2:90, 213, 3:19, 7:33, 10:23, 90, 16:90 42:14, 39, 45:17

Inspire vt Awha أوحى See Reveal

Institution Sunnah سنة

Diverse institutions have passed away before you (3:137)
See also 4:26, 8:38, 15:13, 17:77, 18:55, 33:38, 62, 35:43, 40:85, 48:23

Insult one another Tanabaza تنابز See Revile one another

Intellect Albab ألباب See Mina

Intercessor Shafi' شفيع

> They, apart from God, will have no protector and no intercessor (6:51)
> Apart from Him, you have no protector neither intercessor (32:4)
> See also 6:70, 94,7:53,10:3,18,30:13,39:43,40:18

Interpretation Ta'wil تاويل

> None knows its interpretation, save only God (3:7)
> We know nothing of the interpretation of nightmares (12:44)
> See also 4:59, 7:53, 10:39, 12:6, 21, 36, 37, 45, 100, 101, 17:35,18:78, 82

Intimate friend Bitanah بطانة

> Take not for your intimate friend, these outside of your ranks (3:118)
> See also 55:54

Intoxicated Sukara سكارى See Drunken

Invent Ibtada'a ابتدع

> And monasticism they invented (57:27)

Iram Iram إرم

> Iram of the pillars (89:7)

Iron Hadid حديد

> We sent down iron, wherein is great might (57:25)
> See also 17:50, 18:96, 22:21, 34:10

Isaac Ishaq إسحاق

> Was not Jew or Christian 2:140
> An extra 211:72
> Was the prophet 37:112

Was blessed upon 37:113

Ishmael Ismael إسماعيل

> The God of thy fathers Abraham, Ishmael and Isaac (2:133)
> See also 2:125, 127, 136, 140, 3:84, 4:163, 6:86, 4:163, 6:86, 14:39, 19:54s, 21:85, 38:48

Islam Silm سلم See Peace.

Israel Israel إسرائيل

> Children of 2: 40-86
> Favours 2:47-53, 2:60, 122, 45:16-17
> Conenant 2:54-59, 61, 63-74, 5:71, 7:138-141
> Their relations with Muslims 2:75-79
> Their arrogance 2:80, 88, 91
> Their covenants 2:83, 86, 93, 100, 5:12-13, 75
> Their love of this life 2:96
> Ask for a king 2:246-251
> Divided and rebellious 7:161-171
> Twice warned 17:4-8
> Delivered from enemy 20:80-82
> Origin of the name 29:27
> Given book and leaders 32:23-25, 40:53-54

Issue Aqibah عقبة See End

Issue Tawil تاويل See Interpretation

J

Jacob Yaqub يعقوب

    Jacob was charged 2:132
    Was not Jew or Christian 2:140
    Was revealed to 4:163
    He and his people were blessed upon 12:6
    A need of his 12:68
    An extra gift 19:49, 21:72, 29:27
    His servant 38:45

Jesus Isa عيسى

    A righteous prophet 6:85
    Birth 3:45-47, 19:22-23
    Apostle to Israel 3:49-51
    Disciple 3:52-53, 5:111-115
    Taken up 3:55-58, 4:157-159
    Like Adam 3:59
    Not crucified 4:157
    No more than apostle 4:171, 5:75, 43:59, 63-64
    Not God 5:17,75
    Sent with Gospel 5:46
    Not son of God 9:30
    Message and miracles 5:110, 19:30-33
    Prays for Table of viands 5:114
    Taught no false worship 5:116-118
    Disciples declare themselves Muslims 5:111
    Mission limited 13:38
    Followers have compassion and mercy 57:27
    Disciples as God's helpers 61:14
    As a sign 23:50, 43:61
    Prophesied Ahmad 61:6

Jews Yahudi يهودي

> Will listen to falsehood 5:41-42
> Utter blasphemy 5:82
> Who became Muslims 26:197, 28:53
> And Christians 2:140, 5:18

Jinn Jinn جن

> To every prophet an enemy—Satans of men and jinn (6:112)
> See also 6:100, 128, 130, 7:38, 179, 17:88, 18:50, 27:17, 39 34:12, 41, 41:25, 29, 46:18, 29, 51:56, 55:33, 72:1, 5, 6

Job Ayyub أيوب

> Remember also our servant Job (38:41)
> See also 4:163, 6:84, 2:83, 38:41

John Yahya يحي

> Birth 3:39, 6:85
> His character and position 19:12-15
> Reverenced God 21:90

Jonah Yunus يونس

> Jonah too was one of the Envoys (37:139)
> See also 4:163, 6:86, 10:98

Joseph Yusuf يوسف

> Joseph 6:84
> His story 12:4-101
> His vision 12:4-6
> Jealousy of his brothers 12·7-10
> Their plot 12:11-18
> Sold by his brethren 12:19-20
> Bought by Aziz of Egypt 12:21
> Tempted by Aziz's wife 12:2-29

    Her ruse 12:30-34
    In prison 12:35-42
    Interprets king's vision 12:43-54
    Established in power 12:55-57
    His dealings with his brethren 12:58, 93
    Reunion of whole family 12:94-101

Judaise Hada هاد

    The Jews who listen to falsehood, listen to other folk (5:41)
    See also 2:62, 4:46, 160, 5:44, 69, 6:146, 7:156, 18:11, 27:17, 62:6

Judgement Day Yawm Al-Din يوم الدين

    Earth changed, and men gathered; Book of Deed 18:47-49
    Men surge like waves; trumpet blown; Unbelievers will see and hear 18:99-101
    Sectarian differences to be solved; Distress for lack of faith 19:37-39
    Rejecters of the message will bear a grievous burden 20:100-101
    Trumpet will sound; sinful in terror; interval will seem short 20:102-104
    They will follow the Caller; tramp of their feet; all sounds humbled 20:108
    No Intercession except by permission 20:109
    No fear for the righteous 20:112
    Rejecters will be raised up blind 20:124-127
    Scales of Justice 21:47
    True Promise will approach fulfilment; sobs of Unbelievers; the Good will suffer no grief 21:97-103
    Heavens will be rolled up like a scroll; new creation 21:104

Terrible convulsion; men in drunken riot; Wrath of God 22:1-2

Trumpet is blown; Balance of Good Deeds, heavy or light 23:101-104

Voice of Judgment 23:105-111

Time will seem short 32:112-115

False worship will be exposed 25:17-19

Heavens rent asunder; angels sent down; Dominion wholly for God 25:25-26

Wrong doer's regrets 25:27-30

Terror for evil-doers, not for doer of good 27:83-90

Guilty in despair, no Intercessor 30:12-13

Justice done 36: 51-54

Joy and peace for the Good 36:55-58

Day of sorting out 30:14-16, 37:20-21

Wrong-doers questioned; recriminations 37:22-23

Contrast between the righteous, with sound hearts and those straying in evil 37:88-102

Wrong-doers' arrogances 37:33-36

Retribution for evil 37:37-39

Felicity for servants of God 37:40-61

Tree of Zaqqum 37:62-68

Wrong-doers rushed on their fathers' footsteps 37:69-74

Trumpet, all in heaven and earth will swoon; second trumpet, renewed earth will shine with God's Glory; recompense 36:67-70

No intercession; justice and truth 40:18-20

Sudden; friends will be foes, except the righteous 43:66-67

No fear on God's devotees 43:68-69

Dealers in falsehood to perish; righteous to obtain Mercy 45:27-35

Not to be averted; Fire for the false and the triflers 52:7-16

Wrong-doers swoon in terror 52:45-47

Caller to a terrible affair 54:6-8

No defence for the evil; known by their Marks 55:35-44

Mutual gain and loss 64:9:10

Shin to be laid bare 68:42-43

Truimph Great Event; Angels will bear the throne; nothing hidden; Good and Evil recompensed 69:13-37

Sky like molten brass; no friend will ask friend; no deliverance for evil 70:8, 18

Wicked will issue from sepulchres in haste 70:43-44

Will know reality, not known whether near or far 72:24-25

Children hoary-headed; sky cleft asunder 73:17-18

Trumpet Day of Distress for those without Faith 74:8-10

Stars become dim; apostles collect; sorting out 77:7-15

Woe to Rejecters of Truth 77:29-50

Sorting out; Trumpet; heavens opened; mountains vanish 78:17-20

Spirits and angels stand forth; Day of reality 78:38-40; Commotion and agitation 79:6-9

Single cry 79:13-14

Deafening noise, no one for another; some faces beaming; some dust-stained 80:33-42

Sun, stars, mountain, outer nature change; soul sorted out; World on High unveiled 81:1-14

Sky cleft asunder; stars and oceans scattered; Graves turned upside down; each soul will know its deeds 82:1-5

No soul can do ought for another 82:17-19

Sky and earth changed; man ever toiling on towards his Lord; Record of good or ill 84:1-15

Things secret tested 86:9-10

Overwhelming event; faces humiliated and faces joyful 88:21-30

Earth pounded to powder; Lord comes; hell and heaven shown 89:21-30

Earth in convulsion; man in distress; sorted out 99:1-8
Contents of graves scattered abroad; of human breast made manifest; Lord well acquainted 100:9-11
Noise and clamour; good and evil rewarded 101:1-11

Judgement Din دين

Must come 6:51, 6:128, 34:3-4; 40:59; 51:5-6, 12-14, 52:7-10; 56:1-7; 64:7-10; 95:7
Will come suddenly 7:187, 36:48-50
As the twinkling of an eye 16:77, 54:50
Hour known to God alone 33:63; 67:26, 79:42-46
Is near 54:1-5, 78:40
Men will be sorted out into three classes 56:7-56
Foremost in Faith, nearest to God 56:11-26
Companions of Right Hand 56:27-40
Companions of Left Hand 56:41-56
Lesser judgment 75:22-30, 78:40
The great news 78:1-5
Deniers of 107:1-7

Judgment Furqan فرقان See Salvation

Jugular Vein Warid وريد

We are nearer to him than the jugular vein (50:16)

Just Barr برّ See Pious

Just Stand Qawam قوام

Neither prodigal nor parsimonious, but between that is a just stand (25:67)

Justice Qist قسط

And fill up the measure and the balance with justice (6:152)

And weigh with justice, and skimp not in the Balance (55:9)

Believers, be you securers of justice, witnesses for God (4:135)

See also 3:18, 21, 4:127, 5:8, 42, 7:29, 10:4, 47, 54, 11:85, 21:47, 57:23

Justice Adl عدل See Counterpoise

K

Ka'ba Bayt بيت See House

Keep the Sabbath Sabata سبت

> On the day they kept not Sabath, they came unto them (7:163)

Keep vigil Tahajjda تهجد

> As for the night, keep vigil a part of it (17:79)

Kind Barr برّ See Pious

Kindness Barr برّ See Piety

Kingdom Malakut ملكوت

> We were showing Abraham the kingdom of the heavens and earth (6:75)
> See also 7:185, 23:88, 36:83

Know Dara دری

> No soul knows what it shall earn tomorrow (31:34)
> No soul knows in what land it shall die (31:34)
> Even though I know not whether near or far is that you are promised (21:109)
> I know not what shall be done with me or with you (46:9)
> See also 4:11, 21:111, 42:52, 45:32, 46:9, 65:1, 69:26, 72:10, 25

Know 'Arafa عرف See Recognise

Know vt Alima علم

> Then a soul shall know its works (82:5)
> We have distinguished the signs for a people who want to know (6:97)

See also 2:13, 22, 26, 30,33,42, 60, 65, 75, 77, 78, 80,101,102,103,106,107,113,118, 143,144, 146,151, 169, 184,187, 188, 197, 216, 220, 230, 232, 235, 239,255, 259, 270, 280, 3:7, 29, 66, 71, 75, 78,135, 140,142, 166, 167,4:43, 63, 83, 113, 5:40, 94, 97, 99, 104, 113, 116, 6:3, 33, 37, 50, 59, 60, 66, 81, 91, 97,105, 114, 135, 7:28,32

Knower Alim عليم See All-knowing

Korah Qarun قارون

Now Korah was of the people of Moses (28:76)
See also 28:78, 29:39,40:24

Koraish Quraysh قريش

For the composing of Koraish (106:1)

L

Language Lisan لسان See Tongue

Large tent Suradiq سرادق See Pavilion

Last Day Akhir آخر

We believe in God and the Last Day (2:8)
The Last Abode is better for those that are god-fearing (7:169)
Those who believe in God and the Last Day ask not leave of Thee (9:44)
See also 2:62, 94, 126, 177, 228, 232, 264, 3:72, 114, 4:38, 39, 59, 136, 162, 5:69, 114, 6:32, 9:18, 19, 29, 45, 99, 10:10, 24:2, 26:84, 28:77, 83, 29:36, 64, 33:21, 69, 37:78, 108, 119, 129, 38:7, 43:56, 53:25, 56:14, 40, 49, 57:3, 58:22, 60:6, 65:2, 77:12, 79:25, 92:13, 93:4

Laugh Dahika ضحك

Therefore let them laugh little, and weep much (9:82)
Behold, the sinners were laughing at the believers (83:29)
Today the believers are laughing at the unbelievers (83:34)
See also 11:71, 23:110, 27:19, 43:47, 53:60, 80:39

Lawful Halal حلال

Eat of what is in the earth, lawful and good (16:114)
See also 5:88, 8:69, 10:59, 16:116

Lead astray Adalla أضل

Do you desire to guide him whom God has led astray? (4:88)

Satan desire to lead them astray into far error (4:60)
God leads astray whomsoever He will (13:27)
But they lead only themselves astray (4:113)
See also 2:26, 28, 3:39, 4:60, 88, 113, 119, 143, 5:77, 6:39, 116, 119, 125, 144, 7:38, 155, 178, 186, 9:37, 115, 10:88, 13:27, 33, 14:4, 27, 30,36, 16:25, 37,93, 17:97, 18:17, 51, 20:79, 85, 22:4, 9, 25:17,29, 42, 26:99, 28:15, 30:29, 31:6, 33:67, 35:8, 36:62, 38:26,39:36,37, 40:33, 34, 74, 41:29,42:44, 46, 45:23, 47:1, 4,8, 71:24, 27, 74:31

Leader Imam امام

I make you a leader for the people (2:124)
See also 9:12, 11:17, 15:79, 17:71, 21:73, 25:74, 28:5, 41, 32:24, 36:12, 46:12

Legion Khusr جند See Host

Lend step by step Istadraja إستدرج See Draw on gradually

Lesser offences Lamam لمم

Those who avoid the heinous sins and indecencies, save lesser offences (53:32)

Lesson 'Ibrah عبرة

Surely in that is a lesson for men (8:13)
In the cattle there is a lesson for you (16:66)
See also 12:111, 23:21, 24:44, 79:26

Lice Qummal قمل

We let loose upon them the flood and the locusts, the lice and the frogs (7:133)

Life Amr عمرو

By the life, they wandered blindly (15:72)

Life Hayat حياة See Present life

Life Hayat Mahya حياة، محي

> The present life is but the joy of delusion (3:185)
> See also 2:85, 86, 96, 179, 204, 212, 3:14, 117, 4:74, 94, 109, 6:29, 32, 70, 130, 7:32, 51, 157,9:38, 55, 10:7, 23, 24, 64, 88, 98, 11:15, 13:26, 34, 14:3, 27,16:97, 107, 17:75, 18:28, 45, 46, 104, 2:72,97, 131, 23:33, 37, 24:33, 25:3, 28:60, 61, 79, 29,:25, 64, 30:7,31:33, 33:28 35:5, 39:26, 40:39, 51, 41:16, 31, 42:36,43:32,35, 45:24, 35,46:20, 47:36, 53:29,57:20, 67:2, 79:38, 87:16, 89:24
> For Mahya, My living, my dying–all belongs to God (6:162)
> See also 45:21

Light Diya' ضياء See Radiance

Lighting Barq برق

> He shows you lighting, for fear and hope (30:24)
> The gleam of His lighting snatches away the sight (24:43)
> See also 2:19, 20, 13:12

Lightning Taghiyah طاغية See Screamer

Like Shiah شيعة See Sect

Likeness Mathal مثل See Similitude

Likeness Shakilah شاكلة See Manner

Living Mahya محى

> My living, my dying— all belongs to God (6:162)
> See also 45:21

Load Hamala حمل See Bear

Load Isr إصر

Our Lord, charge us not with a load (2:286)
See also 3:81, 7:157

Locusts Jarad جراد

We let loose upon them the flood and the locusts (7:133)
See also 54:7

Lodging Mawa ماوى See Refuge

Lodging place Mustaqarr مستقر See Sojourn

Lofty Aliy علي See High

Lofty chamber Ghurfah غرفة See Upper Chamber

Lokman Luqman لقمان

Given wisdom (31:12)
Admonishes his son (31:13)

Look for Bagha بغى See Be insolent

Lord Mawali موالي See Protector

Lord Rabb رب

Praise belongs to God, the Lord of all being (1:2)
See also 2:5, 21,26,30,37,46, 49, 61, 62, 68, 69, 70, 76, 105,12, 124, 126, 127, 128, 129, 131,136, 139, 144,147,149,157, 178, 198, 200, 201, 248, 250, 258,260, 262, 274, 275, 277, 282, 283, 285,286, 3:7, 8,9,15, 16, 35, 36, 37,38,40,41, 43, 47, 49, 50, 51, 53, 60, 64, 73, 80, 84,124, 125, 133, 136, 147, 169, 191, 192, 193m, 194, 195, 198, 199, 4:1, 65, 75, 77, 170,174, 5:2, 24, 25,28, 64, 66, 67, 68,72, 83, 184, 12, 14, 117

Lose Heart Fashila فشل

Do not quarrel together, and so lose heart (8:46)
See also 3:122, 152, 8:43

Loss Khusran, Khusr خسران، خسر

> Whoso takes Satan to him for a friend, instead of God, has surely suffered a manifest loss (4:119)
> And such as do corruption in the land – They shall be the losers (2:27)
> See also 2:64, 121, 3:85,149, 4:119, 5:5, 21, 30, 53, 6:12, 20, 31, 140, 7:9, 23, 53, 90, 92, 99, 149,178, 8:37, 9:69, 10:45, 95, 11:21, 22, 47, 12:14, 16:109, 18:103, 21:70, 22:11, 23:34, 103, 27:5, 29:52, 39:15, 65, 40:78, 85, 41:23, 25, 42:45, 45:27, 46:18, 58:19, 63:9, 65:9, 79:12

Lot Lut لوط

> Questioned his nation 7:80, 26:161, 27:54, 29:28
> Angels sent to his nation 11:70, 77, 29:33
> His follower saved 15:59, 21:71
> He was given wisdom and knowledge 21:74
> His nation denied the Messengers 26:160
> He was threatened to be ousted 26:167, 27:56
> He was a Messenger 37:133
> His nation denied warnings 54:33
> A squall of pebbles was loosed against them 54:34
> His wife disobedient 66:10

Loud Jahr جهر

> Be thou not loud in the prayer, nor hushed (17:115)
> God likes not the shouting of evil words (4:148)
> He knows what is spoken aloud and what is hidden (87:7)
> See also 6:3, 7:205, 13:10, 16:75, 17:110, 20:7, 21:110, 49:2, 67:13, 87:7

Love Ahabba أحبّ

> God loves the just (5:42)
> God loves the good-doers (2:195)

God loves those who fight in His way (61:4)

God loves not any ungrateful traitor (22:38)

See also 2:165, 190, 205,216, 222, 276, 3:31, 32, 57, 76, 92, 119 134, 140, 146, 148, 152, 159, 188, 4:36, 107,148, 5:13, 42, 54, 64, 87, 93, 6:76, 141, 7:31, 55, 29, 8:58, 9:108, 16:23,22:38, 24:19, 28:56, 76, 77, 30:45,31:18 38:32, 42:40,49:9, 12, 57:23, 59:9, 60:8, 61:13, 75:20, 76:27, 89:20

Love Hubb حبّ

I have loved the love of good things (38:32)

They give food for the love of Him (76:8)

See also 2:165, 177, 3:14, 12:30,89:20, 100:8

Love Hubb, Mahabbah حب،محبة

I have loved the love of good thing (38:32)

See also 2:165, 177, 3:14, 12:30, 76:8, 89:20, 100:8

For Mahabbah 20:39

Love Mawaddah مودة

He has set between you love and mercy (30:21)

See also 4:73, 5:82, 29:25, 42:23, 60:1, 7

Lovers Akhdan أخدان

Not as in licence or taking lovers (4:25)

See also 5:5

Lower vt Ghadda غض See Cast down

Lump Kisf كسف See Fragment

Lust Hawa هوى See Desire

Lust Shahwah شهوة

Those who follow their lusts desire you to swerve away mightily (4:27)

See also 3:14, 7:81, 19: 59,27:55

M

Magians Majus مجوس

> The Sabaeans, the Christians, the Magians and the idolaters (22:17)

Magnify Sabbaha سبح See Praise

Magog Majuj ماجوج

> Gog and Magog are doing corruption (18:94)
> See also 21:94

Make 'Amila عمل See Do

Make joyful Habara هبر

> Enter Paradise, you and your wives walking with joy (43:70)
> See also 30:15

Make a convenant 'Aahada عاهد

> Fulfil God's convenant, when you make convenant (16:91)
> Men who were true to their convenant with God (33:23)
> See also 2:100, 177, 8:56, 9:1,4,75, 33:15, 48:10

Make a convenant 'Ahida عهد

> God has made convenant with us. (3:183)
> By the convenant He has made with you (43:49)
> See also 2:125, 7:134, 20:115, 36:60, 43:49

Make amends Aslaha أصلح

> Whosoever believes and makes amends—no fear shall be on them (6:48)
> Save such as repent there after and make amends (24:5)

See also 2:11, 160, 182, 220, 224, 228, 3:89, 4:16, 35, 114, 128, 129, 148, 5:39, 6:48, 54, 7:35, 56, 85, 142, 170, 8:1, 10:81, 11:88, 117, 16:119, 21:90, 24:5, 26:152, 27:48, 28:9, 33:71, 42:40, 46:15, 47:2, 5, 49:9, 10

Make an associate Ashraka أشرك See Associate

Make clear manifest Bayyana بيّن

We have indeed made clear for you the signs (57:17)
We have sent down to you signs making all clear (24:34)
See also 2:68, 69, 70, 118, 159, 160, 187, 219, 221, 230, 242, 266, 3:103, 118, 187, 4:19, 20, 176, 5:15, 19,75, 89,6:105, 9:115, 14:4, 16:39, 44, 64, 92, 22:5,24:18,46, 58, 59, 61, 33:30, 43:63, 65:1, 11

Make easy Yassara يسَّر

Now we have made the Koran easy for Remembrance (54:17)
Now we have made it easy by thy tongue (19:97)
We shall surely ease him to the hardship (92:10)
See also 44:58,54:22,32,40,80:20,87:8,52:7

Make provision Razaqa رزق See Provide

Make room vt Fasaha, Tafassaha فسح ، تفسح

Make room in the assemblies (58:11)
For, Tafassaha 58:11

Make subservient Sakhkhara سخّر See Subject

Make the pilgrimage (to Mecca) Hajja حج

Whosoever makes the pilgrimage to the House (2:158)
See also 2:189, 196, 197, 3:97, 9:3, 22:27

Male Dhakar ذكر

The male is not as female (3:36)

He Himself created the two kinds, male and female (53:45)

See also 3:195, 4:11, 124, 176, 6:139, 143, 144, 16:97, 26:165, 40:40, 42:49, 50, 49:13, 53:21, 75:39, 92:3

Malik Malik مالك

"O Malik, would that your Lord, put on end to us!" let thy Lord have done with us (43:77)

Man Ins إنس

Man Bashar بشر See Mortal

Man Insan إنسان

    Vicegerent on earth 2:30, 6:165
    Tested by God 2:155, 3:186, 47:31, 57:25
    One nation 2:213, 10:19
    Things men covet 3:14
    Duty 4:1-36, 17:23-39, 29:8-9, 30:38, 31:33, 46:15, 70:22-35
    Created from clay, for a term 6:2, 15:26
    Called to account 6:44
    Will return to God 6:60, 72, 10:45-56
    Confusion of the wicked at death 6:93-94
    Plots against own soul 6:123, 10:44
    Personal responsibility 6:164
    Ungrateful 7:10; 36: 45-47, 74:15-25, 100:1-8,
    Warned against Satan 7:27
    Knows of God, but misled by Evil 7:172-175
    And family life 7:189-190
    Transgress insolently 10:23
    Limited Free-will 10:99

Behaviour in and out of trouble 10:12, 11:11, 16:53-53 17:67-70, 29:10, 65-66, 30:33-34, 31:32 39:8, 49, 41:49-51, 42:48, 89:15-16

God's spirit breathed into him 15:29

Lowly in origin, but blessed with favours 16:4-8, 32:7-9 35:11, 36:77-78, 76:1-3, 77:20-24, 80:17-32:7-9, 35:11 36:77-78, 76:1-3, 77:20-24, 80:17-32, 86:5-896:2-5

Prays for evil 17:11

Is given to hasty deeds 17:11, 16:37

His fate fastened round his neck 17:13

To be jugded by his record 17:13

Heed not, though Reckoning near 21:1-3

His physical growth 22:5, 23:15-14, 40:67

Death and Resurrection 23:15-16

Tongues, hands, and feet will bear witness against men 24:24

Made from water 25:54

Relationships of lineage and marriage 25:54

Pattern according to which God has made mankind 30:30

Should submit self to God 31:22

Not two hearts in one breast 33:4

To worship God 39:64-66

Misfortunes, due to his deeds 42:30

Honour depends on righteousness 49:13

Angels note his doings 50:17-18, 23

His growth and activity depend on God 56:57-74

To be created again after death in new forms 56:60-61

Riches and family may be a trial 64:14-15

Created and provided for by God 67:23-24, 74:12-15

Is impatient 70:19-21

Who will be honoured once among men 70:22-35

Evidence against himself 75:14-15

His arrogance 75:32-40, 90:5-7

Loves the fleeting world 76:27
Seduced from God 82:6-12
Painfully toiling on to God 84:6
Travels from stage to stage 84:16-19
Guilty of sins 89:17-20
Created into toil and struggle 90:4
Gifted with faculties 90:8-10
Strives for diverse ends 92:4-11
Created in best of moulds 95:4
Abased unless he believes and does righteousness 95:5-6
Transgresses all bounds 96:6-14

Manat Manat مناة

And Manat the third, the other (53:20)

Mankind Bashar بشر See Mortal

Mankind Ins إنس

An enemy— Satan of men and jinn. (6:112)

We have created jinn and mankind except to serve me (51:56)

See also 6:128, 130, 7:38, 17:88, 27:17, 41:25, 29, 46:18, 55:33, 39, 56, 74, 72:5, 6

Manna Mann من

We sent down manna and quails upon you (2:57)
See also 7:160, 20:80

Manner Duniya دنيا See World

Manner Shakilah شاكلة

Every man works according to his own manner (17:84)

Mark Athar أثر See Footstep

Marriage Nikah نكاح

    To unbelievers or slaves 2:221
    To how many, lawful 4:3
    Dower not to be taken back (in case of divorce) 4:20-21
    Prohibited degrees 4:22-24
    If no means to wed free believing women 4:25
    If breach feared, two arbiters to be appointed 4:35
    If wife fears cruelty or desertion, amicable settlement 4:128
    Turn not away from a woman 4:129
    With chaste ones among People of the Book 5:5
    Of adulterers 24:3
    To those who are poor 24:32
    Those who can not afford marriage, to keep themselves chaste until God gives them means 24:33
    Prophet's Consorts, 33:28-29, 50-52, 33:49
    Without cohabitation, no 'Iddat on divorce 33:49
    Conditions for the Prophet 33:50-52, 33:28

Marriage-portion Faridah فريضة See Ordinance

Marry vt Nakaha نكح

    Do not marry woman that your fathers married (4:22)
    Marry such women as seem good to you, two three, four (4:3)
    See also 2:221, 230, 232, 235, 237, 4:3, 6, 22, 25, 24:3, 33, 60, 33:53, 49, 60:10

Martyr Shahid شهيد See Witness

Marut Marut ماروت

    Babylon's two angles, Harut and Marut (2:102)

Marvellous Ujab عجاب

This is indeed a marvellous thing (38:5)

Marwa Marwah مروة

    Safa and Marwa are among the waymarks of God (2:158)

Mary Maryam مريم

    Birth 3:35-37
    Annunciation of Jesus 3:42-51,4:156, 19:16-21
    In child birth 19:23-26
    Brought the babe to her people 19:27-33
    Guarded her chastity 21:91, 66:12

Master Mawla مولى See Protector

Master of religion Habr حبر See Rabbi

Master Rabb رب See Lord

Mate Ba'l بعل

    In such time their mates have better right to restore them. (2:228)
    See also 4:128, 11:72, 24:31, (3).

Meadow Rawdah روضة

    They shall walk with joy in a green meadow (30:15)
    See also 42:22

Mean Wasila وسيلة

    Fear God, and seek the means to come to him (5:35)
    See also 17:57

Means Wasilah وسيلة

    Those they call upon are themselves seeking the means to come to their Lord (17:75)
    See also 5:35

Measure Kayl كيل

And fill up the measure when you measure (17:35)
Fill up the measure and be not cheaters (26:181)
See also 6:152, 7:85, 12:59,60, 63, 65, 88, 83:3

Measure Mikyal مكيال

Diminish not the measure and the balance (11:84)
Fill up the measure and the balance justly (11:85)

Measure Miqdar مقدار

Every thing with Him has its measure (13:8)
See also 32:15, 70:4

Mecca Makah مكة

He who restrained their hands from you, and your hands from them in the hollow of Mecca (48:24)

Meccans Ummy أمي See Illiterate

Mediate upon Tadabbara تدبّر See Ponder

Mediator Qurban قربان See Sacrifice

Mediator Shafi شفيع See Intercession

Medina Madinah مدينة

Some of the people of the city are grown bold (9:101)
See also 7:85, 9:70, 11:84,95,20:40, 22:44, 28:22, 45, 29:36

Men Unas أناس See People

Men of the pit Ukhdud أخدود

Slain where the men of the pit (85:4)

Menstrual period Quru قروء

Divorced women shall wait by themselves for three periods (2:228)

Mention Dhakara ذكر See Remember

Merchandise Tijarah تجارة

> What is with God is better than diversion and merchandise (62:11)
> See also 9, 2:16, 282, 4:29, 9:24, 24:37, 35:29, 61:10

Merchandise Tijarah تجارة See Commerce

Messiah Masih مسيح See Jesus

Meteor Shihab شهاب See Flame

Michael Mikal ميكال

> His angels and His Messengers, and Gabriel, and Michael (2:98)

Middle Wasat وسط See Mid-most

Midian Maydyan مدائن

> When he came to the waters of Midian he found a company of the people 28:23
> See also 7:85, 9:70, 11:84, 95,20:40, 22:44, 28:22, 45, 29:367

Mid-most Wasat وسط

> Thus we appointed you a mid-most nation (2:143)
> See also 2:238, 5:89, 68:28

Might 'Izzah عزّة See Glory

Might Ayd أيد

> And heaven we built it with might (51:47)
> See also 38:17

Might Ba's بأس

> God is stronger in might, more terrible (4:84)

Our might will never be turned back from the people (12:110)

Who will help us against the might of God (40:29)

See also 2:177, 4:84, 6:43, 65, 147, 148, 7:4, 5, 97, 98, 16:81, 17:5, 18:2, 21:12, 80,27:33, 33:18, 40:29,84, 85, 48, 48:16, 57:25, 59:14

Mighty Azim عظيم

Surely with God is a mighty wage (9:22)

See also 2:7, 49, 105, 114, 255, 3:74, 105, 172, 174, 179, 4:13, 27,40, 48, 54, 67, 73, 74, 93,95, 113 114, 146, 156, 162, 5:9, 33, 41,119, 6:15,7:59, 116. 141, 8:28,29, 68,9:20, 22,63, 72, 89, 100,101,111,129, 1:15, 64, 12:28, 14:6,15:87, 1694, 106, 17:40, 19:37, 21:76, 22:1,23:86 24:1, 14, 15, 16, 23, 26, 63, 135, 156, 189, 27:233, 26,28:79, 31:13, 33:29,35, 53,71, 37:76, 107, 115, 38:67,39:13, 40:9, 41:35, 42:4, 43:31, 44:57, 45:10, 46:21, 48:5, 10,29, 49:3,56:46, 74, 76,96,57:10, 12, 21, 29,61:12, 62:4, 64:9, 15, 68:4, 69:33, 52, 73:20,78:2, 83:5

Mind Albab الباب

In retaliation there is life for you, men possessed of minds (2:179)

See also 2:197, 269,3:7, 190,5:100,12:111,13:19, 14:52, 38:29,43, 39:9, 18, 21, 40:54, 65:10

Mind Sadr صدر See Breast

Mingling Amshaj أمشاج

We created man of a sperm-drop, a mingling (76:2)

Mischief Fasad فساد See Corruption

Mysterious letters
    Alif Lam Mim الم

        Alif Lam Mim (2:1)
        See also 3:1, 29:1, 30:1, 32:1

    Alif Lam Mim Ra المر

        See 13:1

    Alif Lam Mim Sad المص

        See 7:1

    Alif Lam Ra الر

        See 10:1, 11:1, 12:1, 14:1, 15:1

    Ayn Sin Qaf عسق

        Ayn Sin Qaf (42:2)

    Nun ن

        Nun, by the pen and what they inscribe (68:1)

    Qaf ق

        Qaf by the glorious Koran (50:1)

Model Imam امام See Leader

Model Uswah أسوة

    You have had a good example in God's Messenger (33:21)
    See also 60:4,6

Modesty Taaffuf تعفف See Abstinence

Molten copper Muhl مهل

    They will be scored with water like molten copper (18:29)
    See also 44:45, 70:8

Monasticism Rahbaniyah رهبانية

> Monasticism they invented; We did not prescribe it for them (57:27)

Monks Ruhban رهبان

> Some of them are priests and monks, and they were not proud (5:82)
> See also 9:31,34

Monstrous Fariy فري

> Thou hast surely committed a monstrous thing (19:27)

Morality Khuluq خلق

> Surely thou art upon a mighty morality (68:4)
> See also 26:137

Mortal Bashar بشر

> I would never bow myself before a mortal (15:33)
> It is He who created of water a mortal (25:54)
> It is naught –but a reminder to mortals (74:31)
> See also 3:47, 74, 5:18, 6:91, 11:27, 12:31, 14:10, 11, 15:20, 16:103, 17:93, 94, 18:110, 19:17,20,26, 21:3, 34, 23:24, 33, 34,47,25:54, 26:154, 30:20, 36:15, 38:71, 41:6, 42:51, 54:24, 64:6, 74:25,29, 36

Moses Musa موسى

> Moses and his people 2:51-61
> Advises Israelites 5:23-29
> Guided by God 6:84
> And Pharaoh 7:103-137,10:75-92,11:96-99, 17:101-103, 20: 43-53, 56-79, 23:45-49, 25:35-36, 26:10-69, 28:4-21, 31-42, 40:23-46, 43:45-56, 51:38-40, 79:156-26
> Resists idol-worship 7:138-141
> Sees the glory on the Mount 7:142-145

Reproves his people for calf worship, amd prays for them 7:148-156

His people 7:159-162

His book, doubts and differences 11:110

To teach his people gratitude 14:5-8

Nine clear signs 7:133, 17:101

To the junction of the two seas 18:60-82

His call 19:51-53, 20:9-56, 28:29-35

His childhood, mother, and sister 20:38-40, 28:7-17

Converts Egyptian magicians 20:70-73, 26:46-52

Indignant at call of worship 20:86-98

And the Fire 27:7-14, 28:29-35

His mishap in the city 28:29-35

In Madyan 28:22-28

Guided to straight way 37:114-122

Books of 53:36, 87:19

Vexed by his people 61:5

Mosque Masjid مسجد

From whatsoever place thou issuest turn thy face towards the Holy Mosque (2:149)

Set your faces in every place of worship and call on Him (7:29)

See also 2:114, 144, 150, 187, 191, 196, 217, 5:2, 7:29, 7:3, 8:34, 9:7, 17, 18, 19, 28, 107, 108, 17:1, 7, 18:21, 22:25, 40, 48:25, 27, 72:18

Most Moderate Wasat وسط See Mid-most

Moulded mud Hama' حمأ

We created man of clay of mud moulded (15:26)

See also 15:28, 33

Mount Tur طور

When we took compact with you, and raised above you the Mount (2:63)

See also 2:93, 4:154, 19:52, 20:80, 23:20, 28:29, 46, 52:1, 95:2

Mountain Jabal جبل

They were hewing the mountains into houses (15:82)

In the mountains are streaks white and red (35:27)

And the mountains shall be like plucked wool tufts (101:5)

See also 2:260, 7:74, 143, 171, 11:42, 43, 13:31, 14:46, 16:68, 81, 17:37, 18:47, 19:90, 20:105, 21:79, 22:18, 24:43, 26:149, 27:88, 33:72, 34:10, 35:27, 38:18, 52:10, 56:5, 59:21, 69:14, 70:9, 73:14, 77:10, 78:7, 20, 79:32, 81:3, 88:19

Muhammad محمد

His mission 7:158, 48:8-9

Respect due to an Apostle 2:104, 4:46

No more than an apostle 3:144

Gentle 3:159

Sent as favour to the Believers 3:164, 4:170

And to the People of the Book 5:19

A mercy to Believers 9:61

Mercy to all creatures 21:107

As a mercy from God 28:46-47, 33:45-48, 36:6, 42:48 72:20-23, 27-28, 76:24-26

His work 3:164, 4:70-71, 6:107, 7:156-157, 10:2, 52:29-34, 74:1-7

Not mad or possessed 7:184, 68:2, 81:22

Warner 7:184, 188 15:89, 53:56-62

Anxious for the Believers 9:128

Brings Message as revealed 10:15-16

His teaching 11:2-4, 12:108, 34:46-50
To deliver revelation entirely as it comes to him 11:12-14, 46:9
God is witness to his mission 13:43, 29:52, 46:8
Heart distressed for men 15:97, 16:127, 18:6, 25:30
To invite and argue, in ways most gracious 16:125-128
Inspired 18:110, 53:2-18
Mocked 25:41-42, 34:7-8
Asks no reward 25:57, 34:47, 38:86, 42:23
His duty 27:91-93, 30:30
His household (consorts) 33:28-34, 50-52, 53, 55, 59, 66:1, 3-6
Close to Believers 33:6
Beautiful pattern of conduct 33:21
Seal of the Prophets 33:40
Universal Messenger to men 34:28
Fealty to him is fealty to God 48:10, 18
Apostle of God 48:29
Resist him not 58:20-22
Foretold by Jesus 61:6
Foretold by Moses 46:10
His Religion to prevail over all religions 61:9
Unlettered 7:157 62:2
Leads from darkness to light 65:11
To strive hard 66:9
Exalted standard of character 68:4
Not a poet or soothsayer 69:40-43
Devoted to prayer 73:1-8, 20, 74:3
Witness 73:15-16
And the blind man 80:1-10
Saw the Angel of Revelation 53:4-18, 81:22-25
To adore God and bring himself closer to him 96:19
Rehearsing scriptures 98:2

Mustard seed Khardal خردل

> Not one soul shall be wronged anything even if it be the weight of one grain of ...(21:47)
> See also 31:16

Muster Hashara حشر

> He shall muster them all together (34:40)
> Had We mustered against them every thing 6:111
> Fear God, unto whom you shall be mustered (5:96)
> See also 2:203, 3:12, 158, 4:172, 5:96, 9:22, 38, 51, 72, 128, 7:111, 8:24, 36, 10:28, 45, 15:25, 17:97, 19:68, 85, 20:59, 102, 124, 23:79, 25:17, 34, 26:53, 27:17, 83, 34:40, 37:22, 38:19, 41:19, 46:6, 50:44, 58:19, 59:2, 67:24

Mutual deceit Dakhal دخل

> Take not your oaths as mere mutual deceit (16:94)
> See also 16:92

N

Nakedness Awrah عورة

> The evening prayer - three times of nakedness for you (24:58)
> See also 24:31, 33:13

Nation Ummah أمة

> The people were one nation (2:213)
> See also 2:128, 134, 141, 143, 3:104, 110, 113, 4:41, 5:48, 66, 6:38, 42, 108, 7:34, 38, 159, 160, 164, 168, 181, 10:19, 47, 49,11:8,48, 118, 12:45, 13:30, 15:5, 16:36, 63, 84, 89, 92, 120, 21:92, 22:34, 67, 23:43, 44, 52, 27:83, 28:23, 75, 29:18, 35:24, 42:5, 41:25, 42:8, 43:22, 23, 33, 45:28, 18

Nearer Duniyah دنيا See World

Neck Raqabah رقبة

> To ransom the slave to perform the prayer (2:177)
> See also 4:92, 5:89, 9:60, 47:4, 58:3, 90:13

Needy Ba 'is بائس See Wretched

Needy Faqir فقير See Poor

Needy Miskin مسكين

> To be good to parents, and the near kinsman, and to the orphan, and to the needy (2:83)
> They give food for the love of Him, to the needy (76:8)
> See also 2:177, 184, 215, 4:8, 36, 5:89, 95, 8:41, 9:60, 17:26, 18:79, 24:22, 30:38, 58:4, 59:7, 68:24, 69:34, 74:44, 89:18, 90:16, 107:3

Neglect Ada 'a أضاع See Waste

Neglect vt Farrata فرط

> We have neglected nothing in the Book (6:38)
> See also 6:31, 12:80, 39:56

New Bid بدع See Innovation

New moon Ahilla أهلة

> They will question thee concerning the new moons (2:189)

Nickname Alqab ألقاب

> Neither revile one another by nicknames (49:11)

Niggardliness Shuhh شح See Avarice

Night Layl ليل

> He subjected to you the night and day (16:12)
> And We appointed the night for a garment (78:10)
> It is God who made for you the night to repose in it (40:61)
> See also 2:51, 164, 187, 274, 3:27, 113, 190, 6:13, 60, 76, 96, 7:54, 142, 10:6, 24, 27, 67, 11:81, 114, 13:3, 10, 14:33, 15:65, 16:12, 17:1, 12,78, 79, 19:10, 20:130, 21:20, 33, 42, 22:61, 23:80, 24:44, 25:47, 62, 27:86, 28:71, 72, 73, 30:23, 31:29, 34:18, 33, 35:13, 36:17, 40, 37:138, 39:5,9, 40:61, 41:37, 38, 44:3, 23,45:5, 50:40, 51:17, 52:49, 57:6, 69:7, 71:5, 73:2, 6, 20, 74:33, 76:26, 79:29, 81:17, 84:17, 89:2, 4, 91:4, 92:1, 93:2, 97:1,2,3

Noah Nuh نوح

> He was chosen 3:33
> Revealed to him 4:163, 6:84
> Sent to his people 7:59, 11:25

Called his son 11:42
Grateful to his Lord 17:3
Denied by his people 22:42, 38:12, 40:5, 50:12
Questioned his people 26:106
Threatened to be stoned 26:116
His stay among his people 29:14
Blessed upon 37:79
Wife unrighteous 66:10
His call against his people 71:2, 26

Nomads Arab عرب

Bedouins came with their excuses (9:90)
See also 9:97,98,99,101,120,33:20,48:11,16,49:14

Non Arab Ajamiy أعجمى

If we had sent it down on a barbarian (26:198)
See also 16:103, 41:44

Number Ahsa أحصى

Every thing We have numbered in a Book (78:29)
God has numbered it and they have forgotten it (58:6)
See also 14:34, 16:18, 18:49, 19:94, 36:12, 65:1, 72:28, 73:20

O

Obey vt Ataa أطاع

Obey God and the Messenger (3:32)
See also 2:285, 3:32, 50, 132, 168, 4:13, 34, 46, 59, 64, 69, 80, 5:7, 92, 6:16, 121, 8:1, 20, 46, 9:71, 18:28, 20:90, 23:34, 24:47, 51, 52, 54, 56, 25:52, 26:108, 110, 126, 131, 144, 150, 151, 163, 179, 29:8, 31:15, 33:1, 33, 48, 66, 67, 71, 40:18, 43:54, 63, 47:26, 33, 48:16, 17, 49:7, 14, 58:13, 64:12, 16, 68:8, 10, 71:3, 76:24, 81:21, 96:19

Observe Hafaza حافظ See Be watchful

Observer Raqib رقيب

Not a word he utters, but by him is an observer ready (50:18)
See also 4:1, 5:117, 11:93, 33:52

Offering Hady هدى

Shave not your heads, till the offering reaches its place (2:196)
See also 5:2, 95, 97, 48:25

Old Atiq عتيق

Place of sacrifice is by the Ancient House (22:33)
See also 22:29

Old age Itiy عتي

I have attained to the declining of old age (19:8)
See also 19:69

Omnipotent Qahhar قهار

God is the Creator of every thing, and He is the One the Omnipotent (13:16)
See also 12:39, 14:48, 38:65, 39:4, 40:16

One Ahad أحد

He is God, One (112:1)
We make no division between any of them (2:136)
Wives of the Prophet; you are not as other women (33:32)
See also 2:96, 102, 180, 266, 282, 285, 3:73, 84, 91, 153, 4:18, 20, 43, 152, 5:6, 20, 27, 106, 115, 6:61, 7:80, 8:7, 9:4, 6, 52, 84, 127, 11:81, 12:36, 41, 78, 15:65, 16:58, 76, 17:23, 18:19, 22, 26, 32, 38, 42, 47, 49, 110, 19:26, 98, 23:99, 24:6, 21, 28, 28:25, 26. 27, 29:28, 35:32, 39, 40, 35:41, 42, 38:35, 43:17, 49:9, 12, 59:11, 63:10, 69:47, 72:2, 7, 18, 20, 22, 26, 74:35, 89:25, 26, 90:5, 7, 92:19, 112:4

One who enjoins Ammar أمار See One who incites

One who incites Ammar أمار

Surely the soul of man incites to evil (12:53)

One who strives to avoid Muajiz معاجز

Those who strive against our signs to avoid them (22:51)
See also 34:5, 38

Open Road Minhaj منهاج

To every one of you we have appointed a right way and an open road (5:48)

Open way Shariah, Shirah شريعة، شرعة

Then We set thee upon an open way of the command (45:18)
To every one of you we have appointed a right way and an open road (95:48)

Opening Farj فرج

    And it has no cracks (50:6)
    See also 21:91, 23:5, 24:30, 31. 33:35, 66:12, 70:29

Oppose 'Asa عصى See Disobey

Oppress vt Zalama ظلم See Wrong

Oppress vt Asa عصى

    The preserving of them oppresses Him not (2:255)

Oratories Qiblah قبلة See Direction of prayer

Ordain Faradh فرض See Appoint

Order vt Amara أمر See Command

Ordinance Faridah فريضة

    God's way, and the traveler; so God ordains (9:60)
    See also 2:23,36, 237, 4:11,24

Ordinances Hudud حدود See bounds

Original Bada'a Abda'a بدأ ، أبدا

    A man of pure faith, God's original (30:30)

Original Fitrah فطرة

    He originated the creation of man (32:7)
    As He originated you so you will return (7:29)
    He made beginning with their sacks (1276)
    See also 9:13, 10:4, 34, 21:104, 27:6,29:20,30:11, 27, 32:6
    See for Abada'a 29:19, 34:49, 85:13

Ornament Zinah زينة See Adornment

Ornaments Hilyah حلية

And bring forth out of it ornaments for you to wear (35:12)

See also 56:67, 68:27, 70:25

Outspread Basata بسط See Stretch out

Overcome vt Ghalaba غلب

If there be twenty of you patient men they will overcome; they will overcome two hundred (8:65)

If God helps you, none can overcome you (3:160)

See also 2:249, 3:12, 160, 4:74, 5:23, 56, 7:113, 8:36, 48, 65, 66, 12:21, 21:44, 26:40, 41, 44, 28:35, 37:116, 173, 41:26, 54:50, 58:21

Overpass Bagha بغى See Be insolent

Overseer Musaytir مسيطر

Thou art not charged to oversee them (88:22)

See also 53:37

Owners of the ditch Ukhdud أخدود See Men of the Pit

P

Parables Amthal امثال

    Man who kindled a fire 2:17-18
    Rain-laden cloud 2:19-20
    Goat-herd 2:171
    Hamlet in ruins 2:259
    Grain of corn 2:261
    Hard barren rock 2:264
    Fertile garden 2:265-266
    Rope 3:103
    Frosty wind 3:117
    Dog who lolls out his tongue 7:176
    Undermined sand-cliff 9:109-110
    Rain and storm 10:24
    Blind and deaf 11:24
    Garden of joy 13:35
    Ashes blown about by wind 14:18
    Goodly trees, with roots, branches, and fruit 14:24-5
    Evil tree 14:26
    Slaves versus man liberally favoured 16:75
    Dumb man versus one who command justice 16:76
    Woman who untwists her yarn 16:92
    City favoured but ungrateful 16:112-113
    Two men, one proud of his possessions and the other absorbed in God 18:32-44
    This life is like rain, pleasant but transitory 18:45-46
    Fall from unity, like being snatched up by birds or carried off by wind 22:31
    A fly 22:73
    Light 24:35-36
    Mirage 24:39

Depths of darkness 24: 40
Spider 29:41
Partners 30:28
Companions of the City 36:13-32
One master and several masters 39:29
Garden promised to the Righteous with kinds of rivers 47:15
Seed growing 48:29
Rain and physical growth 57:20
Mountain that humbles itself 59:21
Donkey 62:5
If stream of water be lost 67:30
People of the Garden 68:17-33

Paradise Firdaws فردوس

The Gardens of paradise shall be their hospitality (18:107)
See also 23:11

Paradise Jannah جنة See Garden

Pardon Ghafara غفر See Forgive

Pardon Ghufran غفران See Forgiveness

Pardon Maghfirah مغفرة See Forgiveness

Pardon vt Afa عفا See Remit

Part Khalaq خلاق See Shara

Partner Shrik شريك See Associate

Party Fi'ah فئة See Host

Party Hizb حزب

Satan's party, surely they are the losers (50:19)

Surely God's party – they are the prosperers (58:22)
See also 5:56, 11:17, 13:36, 18:12, 19:37, 23:53, 30:32, 33:20, 22, 35:6, 38:11, 13, 40:5, 30, 43:65, 58:19, 58:22

Party Shiah شيعة See Sect

Pastures Abb أب

And fruits and pastures (80:31)

Pavilion Suradiq سرادق

We have prepared for the evil-doers a fire, whose pavilion incompasses them (18:29)

Payment Ada أداء

And let the payment be with kindliness 2:178

Peace Salam سلام

God guides whosoever follows His good pleasure in the ways of peace (5:16)
Enter you then, in peace and security (15:46)
They shall receive therein a greeting and peace (25:75)
See also 4:94, 6:54, 127, 7:46, 10:10, 25, 11:48, 69, 13:24, 14:23, 15:46, 52, 16:32, 19:15, 33, 47, 62, 20:47, 21:69, 25:63, 27:59, 28:55, 33:44, 36:58, 37:79, 109, 120, 130, 181, 39:73, 43:89, 50:34, 51:25, 56:26, 91, 59:23, 97:5

Peace Silm سلم

O believers, enter into peace, all of you (2:208)

Peer Andad أنداد See Compares

Pentateuch Tawrat توراة See Torah

Pentent Awwab أواب

He is all-forgiving to those who are pentent (17:25)

See also 38:17, 19, 30, 44, 50:32

People 'Abd عبد See Servant

People Unas أناس

>Surely they are folk that keep themselves clean (7:82)
>On the day when We shall call all men with their record. (17:71)
>See also 2:60, 7:160, 27:56

Perdition Tahlukah تهلكة

>Cast not yourselves by your own hands into destruction (2:195)

Perform vt Ata أعطى See Give

Peril Ba's بأس See Might

Perish Halaka هلك

>All things perish except His face (28:88)
>That whosoever perished might perish by a clear sign (8:42)
>See also 4:176, 8:42, 40:34, 69:29

Permit Ahalla أحل

>Forbid not such good things as God has permitted you (5:87)
>We have made lawful for thee thy wives (33:50)
>The good things are permitted to you (5:4)
>See also 2:187, 275, 3:59, 4:24, 160, 5:1, 4,5, 87, 95, 7:157, 9:37, 22:30, 66:1

Persecution Fitnah فتنة See Trial

Persist vt Sabara صبر See Endure patiently

Pharaoh Firawn فرعون

    Cruelty 2:49
    Drowned 2:50
    People of 54:41-42
    Dealing with Moses 7:103-137, 10:75-92
    Body saved, on account of repentance 10:90-92
    Denies God 28:38, 79:244
    A man from his people confesses Faith 40:28-44
    Arrogant to the Israelites 44:17-33
    Wife righteous 66:11
    Sin and disobedience 69:9, 73:16, 85:17-20, 89:10-14

Physical Maturity Ashudd أشد See Coming of age

Piece Kisf كسف See fragments

Piercing Hadid حديد See Guardian

Piety Barr برّ

    But piety is to be godfearing (2:189)
    Help one another to piety and godfearing (5:2)
    See also 2:44, 177, 189, 3:92, 58:9

Pillar 'Imad عماد

    God is He who raised up the heavens without pillars (13:2)
    See also 31:10, 89:7, 104:9

Pious Barr برّ

    Take us to thee with the pious (3:193)
    Surely the pious shall be in bliss (83:22)
    Surely the pious shall drink of a cup (76:5)
    See also 3:198, 19:14, 32, 52:28, 82:13, 83:18

Pitch into Da' a دع See Repulse

Place of sacrifice Mahill محل

> Their lawful place of sacrifice is by the Ancient House (22:33)
> See also 2:196, 48:25

Place of return Maab ماب See Resort

Place of sacrifice Mahill محلة

> Till the offering reaches its place of sacrifice (2:196)
> See also 3:156, 5:50 , 33:33

Place of safety and security Mafaz مفاز

> For the godfearing awaits a place of security (78:31)

Plank lawh لوح See Tablet

Plastic Lazib لازب See Clinging

Poet Shair شاعر

> And the poets - the perverse follow them (26:224)
> It is not the speech of a poet (69:41)
> See also 21:5, 37:36, 52:30

Poetry Shir شعر

> We have not taught him poetry: it is not seemly for him (36:69)

Polluted Asana أسن See Staling

Pomegranates Rumman رمان

> Gardens of vines, olives, pomegranates (6:99)
> See also 6:141, 55:68.

Ponder Tadabbara تدبّر

> Do they not ponder over the Koran (4:82)

That men possessed of minds may ponder its signs (38:29)

See also 23:68, 47:24

Poor Faqir فقير

If they are poor, God will enrich them of His bounty (24:32)

The free will offerings are for the poor and needy (9:60)

If you conceal them, and give them to the poor, that is better for you (2:271)

Whether the man be rich or poor, God stands closest to either (4:135)

See also 2:273, 3:181, 4:6, 22:28, 28:24, 35:15, 47:38, 59:8

Poor Miskin مسكين See Needy

Poor-due Zakat زكاة

Give poor-due 2:43, 83, 110

He gave poor-due 2:177

They gave poor-due 2:277, 4:77

It will be registered for the doers of poor-due 7:156

Its doers are religious brothers 9:11

He advised me to give poor-due 19:31

It was revealed 19:55

Its givers are the best-men 24:37

It is only for the sake of Allah 30:39

It is a good debt to Allah 73:20

It's a part of the two basic things of the religion 98:5

Portion Dhanb ذنب See Sin

Portion Khalaq خلاق See Share

Postpone vt Akhkhara آخر See Defer

Postponing the month Nasi نسئ

    The month postponed is an increase of unbelief (9:37)

Postponement of (a sacred) **month** Nasi نسئ

    The month postponed is an increase of unbelief (9:37)

Prostrate oneself Sajada سجد See Bow down

Potter's clay Fakhar فخار See Earthen ware

Poverty Khasasah خساسة

    Preferring others above themselves, even though poverty be their portion (59:9)

Poverty Aylah عيلة

    If thou fear poverty, God shall surely enrich you of His bounty (9:28)

Poverty Imlaq إملاق

    And not to slay your children because of poverty (6:151) See also, 17:31

Poverty vt. 'Aylah عيلة

    If thou fear poverty, God shall surely enrich you of His bounty (9:28)

Power 'Izzah عزّة See Glory

Power Rih ريح See Wind

Powerful Matin متين See Sure

Praise vt Sabbaha سبح

    They chant His praise and to Him they bow (7:206)
    All that is in the heavens and the earth magnifies God (57:1)

See also 2:30, 3:41, 13:13, 15:98, 17:44, 19:11, 20:33, 130, 21:20, 79, 24:36, 41, 25:58, 32:15, 33:42, 37:143, 39:75, 42, 40:7, 55, 41:38, 48:9, 50:39, 40, 52:48, 56:74, 96, 59:1, 24, 61:1, 62:1, 64:1, 68:28, 69:52, 76:26, 87:1, 110:3

Pray Da'a دعا See Call

Prayer Da'wah دعوة See Call

Precaution Hidhr حذر

O believers, take your precautions (4:71)
Lay aside your weapons; but take your precautions 4:102

Prefer Faddala فضّل

I have prefered you above all beings (2:47)
Some We have prefered above others (2:253)
God has prefered in rank those who struggle (4:95)
See also 2:122, 4:32, 34. 95, 6:86, 7:140, 13:4, 16:71, 17:21, 55, 70, 27:15, 45:16

Prefer vt Athara أثر

Preferring others above themselves (59:9)
See also 12:91, 20:72, 79:38, 87:16

Preparation Uddah عدة

They would have made some preparation for it (9:46)

Present Hadiyah هدية

Now I will send them a present (27:35)
See also 27:36

Present life Dunya دنيا See World

Present life Hayat حياة

The present life is naught but a sport (57:20)

Who created death and life that He might try you (67:2)

The present life is naught but a diversion (29:64)

See also 2:85, 86, 96, 179, 204, 212, 3:14, 117, 185, 4:74, 94, 109, 6:29, 32, 70, 130, 7:32, 51, 152, 9:38, 55, 10:7, 23, 24, 64, 88, 98, 11:15, 13:26, 34, 14:3, 27, 16:97, 107, 17:75, 18:28, 45, 46, 104, 20:72, 97, 131, 23:33, 37, 24:34, 25:3, 28:60, 61, 79, 29:25, 64, 30:7, 31:33, 33:28, 35:5, 39:26, 40:39, 51, 41:16, 31, 42:36, 43:32, 35, 45:24, 35, 45:24, 35, 46:20, 47:36, 53:29, 57:20, 67:2, 79:38, 87:16, 89:24

Press vt. Ahfa أحفى

If he asks you for them and presses you (47:37)

Prevail over vt Damagha دمغ

We hurt the truth against falsehood and it prevails over it (21:18)

Prevail vt Ghalaba غلب See Overcome

Prick vt. Azza ّعز

How We sent the Satan against the unbelievers, to prick them (19:83)

See also 19:83

Prison Hasir حصير

We have made Gehenna a prison for the unbelievers (17:8)

Prisoner Asir أسير See Captive

Private parts (of males and females) Farj فرج See Opening

Proclamation Adhan أذان

A proclamation from God and His Messenger (9:3)

Prodigal Musrif مسرف

    Be you not prodigal :God loves not the prodigals (6:141)
    Obey not the commandment of the prodigal (26:151)
    See also 5:32, 7:31,81, 10:12, 83, 21:9, 36:19, 40:28, 34, 43, 43:5, 44:31, 51:34

Produce Halumma هلم See Come

Produce Ukul أكل

    Palm-trees and crops diverse in produce (6:141)
    See also 2:265, 13:4, 35,14:25, 18:33.34:16

Prohibit vt Naha نهى See Forbid

Prohibited Haram حرام See Holy

Promise vt Wa'ada واعد

    Unto each God has promised the reward most fair (57:10)
    Satan promises you poverty, and bids you into indecency (2:268)
    See also 3:153, 194, 4:95, 120, 122, 5:9, 6:33, 7:44, 70, 77, 8:7, 9:68, 72, 77, 111, 114, 10:4, 46, 48, 55, 11:32, 45, 65, 13:31, 35, 40, 14:22, 47, 61,16:38, 17:5, 7, 104, 108, 18:21, 98, 109, 22:47, 55, 72, 23:35, 36, 93, 95, 24:55, 25:16, 26:206, 27:71, 28:13,61,30:6, 60, 33:12, 22, 34:29, 35:5, 40, 36:48, 52, 63, 38:53, 39:20, 40:8, 28, 55, 77, 41:30, 43:42, 83, 46:16,17,22,35,47:15, 48:20, 29, 50:32, 51:5, 22, 60, 57:10, 67:25, 70:42,44, 72:24, 25, 73:18, 77:7

Proof Burhan برهان

    Another god where of he has no proof (23:117)
    Produce your proof if you speak truly (2:111)
    See also 4:174, 12:34, 21:24, 27:64, 28:32,75

Property Mal مال See Goods

Prophecy Nubuwah نبوة See Prophethood

Prophet Nabiy نبي

> They had disbelieved the signs of God and slain the Prophet (2:61)
> We have appointed to every Prophet, an enemy (6:112)
> We have preferred some Prophets over others (17:55)
> See also 2:91, 136, 177, 213, 246, 247, 248, 3:21, 39, 68, 80, 81, 84, 112, 146, 161, 181, 4:69, 155, 163, 5:20, 44, 81, 6:112, 7:94, 157, 158, 8:64, 65, 67, 70, 9:61, 73, 113, 117, 17:55, 19:30, 41, 49, 51, 53, 54, 56, 58, 22:52, 25:31, 33:1, 6, 7, 13, 28, 30, 32, 38, 40, 45, 50, 53, 56, 59, 37:112, 39:69, 43:6, 7, 59:2, 60:12, 65:1, 66:1, 3, 8, 9

Prophethood Nubuwah نبوة

> We gave the Children of Israel, the Book, the Judgment and the Prophethood (45:16)
> See also 3:79, 6:89, 29:27, 57:26

Prosper vt Anjaha أنجح

> Come to houses by their doors, and fear God; haply so you will prosper (2:189)
> See also 2:5, 189, 3:104, 130, 200, 5:35, 90, 100, 6:21, 135, 7:8, 69, 157, 8:45, 9:88, 10:17, 69, 77, 12:23, 16:116, 18:20, 20:69, 22:77, 23:102, 17, 24:31, 51,28,:37, 67, 82, 30:38, 31:5, 58:22, 59:9, 62:10, 64:16

Prostrate Sajada سجد See Bow down

Prostrate vt Rakaa ركع

> Prostrate yourselves (77:48)
> 'O men, bow you down and prostrate yourselves (22:77)

See also 2:43, 125, 3:43, 5:55, 9:112, 22:26, 38:24, 48:29, 77:48

Protect Ajara أجار

From God shall protect me not any one (72:22)
Then who will protect the unbelievers from a painful chastisement (67:28)
See also 9:6, 23:88, 46:31

Protector Mawla, Wali مولى، ولي

Have mercy on us, thou art our Protector (2:285)
See also 3:150, 4:33, 6:62, 8:40, 9:51, 10:30, 16:76, 19:5, 22:13, 78, 33:15, 44:41, 47:11, 57:15, 66:2,4
For Wali, God is the Protector of the believers (3:68)
See also 2:107, 120, 257, 282, 122, 175, 4:45, 75, 76, 89, 119,123,139, 144, 173, 5:51,55, 57, 81, 6:14, 51, 70, 121, 127, 128, 7:3, 27, 30, 155, 196, 8:34, 72, 73, 9:23,71, 74, 116, 10:62,11:20, 113,12:101, 13:16, 16:63, 17:33, 97, 18:17, 26, 50, 102, 19:5, 45, 25:18, 27:49, 29:22, 41, 32:4, 33, 6, 17, 65, 34:41, 39:3, 41:31, 34, 42:6, 8, 9, 28, 31, 44, 46, 46:32, 48:22, 60:1, 62:6

Proud Mukhtal مختال

God loves not the proud and boastful (4:36)
See also 31:18, 57:23

Prove vt Ibtala ابتلى See Test

Provide vt Razaqa رزق

Expend of that we have provided them (2:3)
God is He that created you, then He provided for you (30:40)
See also 2:22, 25, 57, 60, 126, 172, 212, 233, 254, 3:27, 37, 4:5, 8, 39, 5:88, 114, 6:140, 142, 151, 7:50, 160, 8:3, 4, 26, 74, 10:31, 59, 93, 11:6, 88, 12:37, 13:22, 26, 14:31,

32, 15:20, 16:56, 67, 71, 72, 73, 75, 112, 114, 17:30, 31, 70, 18:19, 19:62, 20:81, 131, 132, 22:28, 34, 50, 58, 23:72, 24, 26, 38, 27:64, 28:54, 57, 82, 29:17, 60, 62, 30:28, 37, 40, 32:16, 33:31, 34:4, 15, 24, 36, 39, 35:3, 29, 36:47, 37:41, 38:54, 35:52, 40:13, 40:13, 40, 64, 42:12, 19, 27, 38, 45:5, 16, 50:11, 51:22, 57, 56:82, 62:11, 63:10, 65:3, 7, 11, 67:11, 15, 21, 85:16

Psalms Zabur زبور

And we gave to David Psalms (4:163)
See also 3:184, 16:44, 17:55, 21:105, 26:196, 35:25, 54, 53

Punish vt Adhdhaba عذب

Punishment Adhab عذاب

There awaits them a painful chastisement (2:10)
Guard us against the chastisement of the Fire (3:16)
See also 2:7, 49, 85, 86, 90, 96, 104, 114, 126, 162, 165, 166, 174, 175, 178, 201, 3:4, 16, 21, 56, 77, 88, 91, 105,106,176,177,178,181,188,191,4:14,18,25,37, 56, 93, 102,138, 147, 151, 161, 173, 5:33, 36, 37, 41, 73, 80,94,114, 6:15, 30, 40, 47, 49, 65,70,93, 124, 157, 7:38, 39, 59, 73, 141, 156, 164, 165, 167, 8:14

Punishment Iqab عقاب See Retribution

Punishment Nakal نكال

We made it a punishment exemplary for all the former times and for the latter (2:66)
See also 5:38, 79:25

Purify vt Zakka زكّى

Only God purifies whom He will (4:49)

Teach them the Book and Wisdom, and purify them (2:129)

See also 2:151, 174, 3:77, 4:49, 24:21, 53:32, 62:2, 91:9

Push Da' a دع See Repulse

Put in order Aslaha أصلح See Make amends

Put one's trust in Tawakkala توكل See Trust

Put to flight Hazama هزم See Route

Q

Qible Qiblah قبلة See Direction of Prayer

Quails Salwa سلوى

    And we sent down manna and quails upon you (2:57)
    See also 7:160, 20:80

Quarreller Ghawiy غوى

    Moses said to him, "Clearly thou art a quarreller" (28:18)

Quicken Ahya أحى See Give life

Qur'an Qur'an القرآن

    Cannot be produced by other than divine agency, 2:23, 10:38, 11:13
    Inspired Message 4:82, 6:19
    Verses, fundamental and allegorical, 3:7, 11:1
    God is witness 6:19
    God's revelation 6:92, 17:105-107, 27:6, 45:2
    Follow it and do right 6:155
    Respect and attention due to 7:204-206
    Book of Wisdom 10:1, 31:2, 36:2
    In Arabic 12:2, 13:37, 41:44, 42:7, 43:30
    Described 13:31, 36-37, 14:1, 56:77-80
    Makes things clear 15:1, 25:33, 26:2, 27:1, 28:2, 36:69-70, 43:2
    Not to be made into shreds 15:91
    Purpose of revelation 16:64-65
    Language pure Arabic 16:103
    Good news and warning 17:9-10
    And the unbelievers 17:45-47
    Healing and mercy 17-82

Explains similitudes 17:89, 18:54, 39:27
No crookedness therein 18:1-2
Teaching 18:2-4, 19:97, 20:2-7, 26:210-220
Easy 19:97, 44:58, 54:17, 20, 32, 40
Revealed in stages 17:106, 25:32, 76:23, 87:6-7
My people took it for nonsense 25:30
Solves Israel's controversies 27:76
Recite Qur'an 73:4; and pray 29:45
Carries own evidence 29:47-49, 51
Guide and mercy 31:3
Truth from God 32:3, 35:31
Beautiful Message consistent with itself 39:23
Instructs mankind 39:41, 80:11-12
No falsehood can approach it 41:42
Same Message to earlier prophets 41:43, 43:44-45
Not sent to worldly leaders 43:31-32
Seek earnestly to understand 47:24
Admonish with 50:45
Taught by God 55:1-2
To be received with humility 59-21
How to be read and studied 2:121, 75:16-18
In books of honour and dignity 80:13-16
Message to all the Worlds 81:26-29
Unbelievers reject it 84:24-25
Tablet Preserved 85:21-22

R

Rabbi Habr حبر

> They have taken their rabbis and their monks as lords (9:31)
> See also 5:44,63, 9:34

Rack Hajar حجر See Stone

Radiance Diya ضياء

> It is He who made the sun a radiance (10:5)
> See also 21:48, 28:71

Raging (wind) Sarsar صرصار See Clamorous

Rain Ghayth غيث

> He sends down the rain (31:34)
> See also 42:28, 57:20

Raise up Ba 'atha بعث See Send forth

Raise vt Hashara حشر See Muster

Ramadan Ramadan رمضان

> The month of Ramadan, wherein the Koran was sent down to be a guidance (2:185)

Ramparts Araf أعراف

> On the Ramparts are men knowing each by their mark (7:46)
> See also 7:48

Rancour Ghill غل

> Put thou not into our hearts any rancour towards those who believe (59:10)

See also 7:43, 15:47

Rank Darajah درجة

> God will raise up in degrees whom We will (6:83)
> God will raise up in rank those of you who believe (58:11)
> And has raised some of you in rank above others (6:165)
> Surely the world to come is greater in ranks (17:21)
> See also 2:228, 253, 3:163, 4:95, 96, 6:132, 8:4, 9:20, 12:76, 20:75, 40:15, 43:32, 46:19, 57:10

Ransom Fidyah فدية

> No ransom shall be taken from you (57:15)
> See also 2:184, 196

Ransom vt Fada Iftada فدى ، افتدى

> Then set them free, either by grace or ransom (47:4)
> See also 37:107
> For Fada, If they come to you as captives, you ransom them (2:85)
> For Iftads, the sinner will wish that he might ransom himself from the chastisement (70:11)
> See also 2:229, 3:91, 5:36, 10:54, 13:18, 39:47

Requital Iqab عقاب See Retribution

Rash Ashir أشر See Impudent

Ravine Fajj فج

> We set in it ravines to serve as ways (21:31)
> See also 22:27, 71:20

Ready Atid عتيد

> This is what I have made ready (50:23)
> See also 50:18

Rebel Asa عصى See Disobey

Reckoning Hisab حساب

> God is swift at the reckoning (2:202)
> Nothing of their account falls upon those that are god fearing (6:52)
> See also, 2:212, 3:19, 27, 37, 119, 5:4, 6:69, 10:5, 13:18, 21, 40, 41, 14:41, 51, 17:12, 21:1, 23:117, 24:38, 39,26:113, 38:16, 26, 39, 53, 39:10, 40:17, 27, 40, 65:8, 69:20, 26, 78:27, 36, 84:8, 88:26

Recognise 'Arafa عرف

> As they recognise their sons (2:144)
> They recognise the blessing of God (16:83)
> The sinners shall be known by their mark (55:41)
> See also 2:89, 146. 178, 180, 228, 229, 231, 232, 234, 235, 236,240, 241, 263, 273, 3:104, 110, 114, 4:5,6,8, 19, 25, 114, 5:83, 6:20, 7:46, 48, 157, 9:67, 71, 12:58, 62, 16:83, 22:41,72, 23:69, 24:53, 27:93,31:15,17,33:6,32, 59, 47:21, 30,55:41,60:12, 65:2,6, 83:24

Recompense Jaza جزاء

> Their recompense is that there shall rest on them the curse (3:87)
> Their recompense is with their Lord (98:80
> See also 2:48, 123, 191, 3:87, 136, 144, 145, 4:93, 123, 5:29, 33, 38, 85, 95, 6:84, 93, 120, 138, 139, 146, 150, 160, 7:40, 41, 147, 152, 180, 9:26, 82, 95, 121, 10:13, 27, 52, 12:22, 25, 74, 75, 88, 14:51, 16:31, 96, 97, 17:63, 98,

20, 18:88, 106, 20:15, 17, 76, 21:29, 23:111, 24:38, 25:15, 75, 28:14, 25, 84, 29:7, 30:45, 31.33, 32:17, 33:24, 34:4, 33, 37, 35:36, 36:54, 80, 105, 110, 121, 131, 39:34, 35, 40:17, 40, 41:27, 28, 42:40, 45:14, 22, 28, 46:14,20, 52:16, 53:31, 41, 54:14, 35, 55:60, 56:24, 59:17, 66:7, 76:9, 12, 22, 77:44, 78:26, 36, 92:19, 98:8

Record Imam إمام See Leader

Recorder Sijill سجل See Scroll

Recorders Hafazah حفظة

    He sends recorders over you (6:61)

Recourse Mustaquar مستقر See Sojourn

Redemption Fidyah فدية See Ransom

Reflect Tafakkara تفكر

    Surely in that are signs to you; haply you will reflect (2:219)
    We strike them for men, haply they will reflect (59:21)
    See also 2:266, 3:191, 6:50, 7:174, 184, 10:24, 13:3, 16:11, 44, 69, 30:8, 21, 34:46, 39:42, 45:13

Refuge Mawa مأوى

    Surely Paradise shall be the refuge (79:41)
    Whose refuge is Gehenna; An evil home coming (3:162)
    See also 3:151, 197, 4:97, 121, 5:72, 8:16, 9:73, 95, 10:8, 13:18, 17:97, 24:57, 29:25, 32:19, 20, 45:34, 53:15, 57:15, 66:9, 79:39, 41

Refuse Ghutha غثاء See Scum

Register Imam إمام See Leader

Registrar Musaytir مسيطر See Overseer

Reject vt Ankara أنكر See Deny

Reject vt. Kaffara كفر See Disbelieve

Religion Din الدين

    No compulsion in 2:256
    Of Islam 3:19-20, 83-84
    No excesses in 4:171, 5:77-81
    Perfected 5:3
    Not play and amusement 6:70
    Do not divide and make sects 6:159, 30:32
    Universal 13:13-15
    No difficulties imposed in 22:78
    Standard religion is to establish pattern according to which God has made man 30:30
    Same for all prophets 42:13-15
    Ancestral 43:22-24
    Right way of 45:18

Religion Ummah امة See Nation

Remainder Baqiyah بقية

    God's remainder is better for you (11:86)
    See also 2:248, 11:116

Remember Dhakara ذكر

    And they will not remember, except that God wills (74:56)
    So remember Me and I will remember you (2:152)
    And remember God's blessing upon you (33:9)
    See also 2:40, 47, 63, 114, 122, 152, 198, 200, 203, 231, 235, 235, 239,3:41, 58, 103, 135, 191, 4:142, 5:4,7, 11,

20,91,110, 6:118, 119, 121, 138,7:63, 69, 74, 86, 171,
205, 8:26, 45, 12:42, 85, 104,13:28,14:6, 15:6, 16:43,44,
18:24, 28, 63,70,83,101,19:2,16, 41, 35, 51, 54, 56, 67,
20:14, 34, 42,99,113,124,21:2,7, 10, 24, 36, 42, 48, 50,
60, 105, 22:28, 34, 35, 36, 23:71, 110, 24:37, 25:18, 29,
26:5, 29:45, 33:9, 34, 35, 41, 34:3, 36:11, 69, 37:3, 13,
168, 38:1, 8, 17,32,41,45,48,49,57, 87, 39:22, 22, 27, 45,
40:44,41:41, 43:5, 13,36, 44, 46:21, 47:20,53: 29, 54:17,
22, 25,32, 40, 57:16, 58:19, 62:9,10,63:9, 65:10, 68:51,52
72:17, 73:8, 74:56, 76:125, 77:5, 81:27, 94:4

Remember Iddakara إدكر

Is there any that will remember? (54:15)
See also 12:45, 54:22,32,40,51

Reminder Dhikra Tadhkirah ذكرى، تذكرة

In that is a reminder for men possessed of minds (39:21)
And a reminder to every penitent servant (50:8)
Therefore remind, if the Reminder profits (87:9)
See also 6:68, 69, 90, 7:2, 11:114, 120, 21:84, 26:209,
29:51, 38:43, 46, 39:21,40:54, 44:13, 47:18, 50:8,37,
51:55, 74:31, 79: 43, 80:4, 87:9,89: 23
For Tadhkirah 20:3, 56:73, 69:12, 48, 73:19, 74:49, 54,
76:29, 80:11

Remit vt Afa عفا

Yet that you should remit is nearer to godfearing (2:237)
Let them pardon and forgive (24:22)
See also 2:52, 109, 178, 187, 219, 386, 3:134, 152, 155,
159, 4:99, 149, 153, 5:15, 95, 101, 7:95, 199, 9:66, 42:25,
30, 34, 40, 64:14

Remnant Atharah أثارة

Bring me a Book before this or some remnant of a knowledge (46:4)

Remnant Baqi Baqiyah بقية ، باقي See Enduring

Render powerful A 'azza أعز See Exalt

Rent Futur فطور See Fissure

Repent vt Hada هاد See Judaise

Repentance Hitah حطة See Humility

Repository Mustawda مستودع

> He knows its lodging place and its repository (11:6)
> See also 6:98

Reproach Lawmah لومة

> Men who struggle in the path of God, not fearing the reproach of any reproacher (5:54)

Repulse Da'a دع

> That is he who repulse the orphan (107:2)
> The day when they shall be pitched into the fire Gehenna (52:13)
> See also 52:13

Rescue vt Najja نجى See Deliver

Resort Maab مأب

> But God - with Him is the fairest resort (3:14)
> See also 13:29, 36, 38:25, 40, 49, 55, 78:22, 39

Restrain Kaffa كف

> He who restrained their hands from you (48:24)
> Restrain your heads and perform the prayer (4:77)
> See also 4:84, 91, 5:11, 110, 21:39, 48:20

Result Ta'wil تاويل See Interpretation

Resurrection Qiyamah قيامة

> He will surely gather you on the Resurrection Day (6:12) God shall decide between them on the Day of Resurrection (2:113)
> See also 2:85,174, 112, 3:55, 77, 161, 180, 185, 194, 4:87,109, 141, 159, 5:14, 36, 64, 6:12, 7:32, 167,172, 10:60, 98, 99, 16:25, 27, 92,124, 17:13, 58, 62, 97, 18:105,19:95, 20:100,124,21:47, 22:9, 17, 69, 23:16, 25:69, 28:41, 42,61, 71, 72,29:13, 25,35:14, 39:15, 24, 31, 47, 60, 67, 41:40, 42,:45,45:17, 26, 46:5, 58:7, 60:3, 68:39, 75:1, 6

Retaliation Qaisas قصاص

> In retaliation there is life for you (2:179)
> See also 2:178, 2:194,5:45

Reveal vt Nazzala نزل See Send Down

Revelation Kalimah كلمة See Word

Revelation Wahi الوحي

> Doubts solved 2:23
> Of Moses and Jesus 2:87
> Abrogated or forgotten 2:106
> Guidance 3:73
> To prophet and those before him 5:48
> Word that distinguishes Good from Evil 86:11-14
> Do not entertain doubt 6:114; 11:17
> Purpose of 7:2, 203
> In stages 16:101
> Through the Holy Spirit 16:102-3, 26:192-99
> To be proclaimed 96:1

Nature of 41:2-4, 69:50-51, 81:15-21

Revenue Kharaj خراج See Tribute

Reverting Awwab أواب See Pentent

Revile vt Tanabaza تنابز

Find no fault with one another, neither revile one another (49:11)

Revive Ahya أحى See Give life

Reward Uqba عقبى See End

Reward Ajr أجر See Wage

Reward Jaza جزاء See Recompense

Rich Ghaniy غني

If any man is rich, let him be abstinent (4:6)
God was in no need of them. And God is All-sufficient (64:6)
See also 2:263, 267, 273, 3:97, 181, 4:131, 135, 6:133, 9:93, 10:68, 14:8, 22:64, 27:40, 29:6, 31:12, 26, 35:15, 39:7, 47:38, 57:24, 59:7, 60:6, 64:6

Riches Mal مال See Goods

Right way Shirah شرعة See Open way

Righteousness Barr بر See Piety

Righteousness Taqwa تقوى See Godfearing

Rise Hashara حشر See Muster

Ritual sacrifice Nusuk نسك

Then redemption by last, or freewill offering, or ritual sacrifice (2:196)

See also 6:162, 22:67

Rival Andad أنداد See Compeer

Roadway Imam إمام See Leader

Romans Rum روم See Greeks

Route vt Hazama هزم

> A very host of parties is routed there (38:11)
> See also 2:251, 54:45

Ruggedness Amt أمت See Curving

Ruler Musaytir مسيطر See Overseer

Runner (with out-stretched neck) Muhti مهطع

> When they shall run with necks out-stretched?
> See also 54:8, 70:36

S

Sabbath Sabat سبت

    The Sabbath was only appointed for those who were at variance thereon (16:124)
    See also 2:65, 4:47, 154, 7:163

Sacred Haram حرام See Sacred

Sacred monument Mashar مشعر See Waymark

Sacred things Hurumat حرمات See Holy things

Sacred visitation to Mecca 'Umrah عمرة

    Fulfil the pilgrimage and the visitation unto God (2:196)
    See also 2:196

Sacrifice Hady هدي See Offering

Sacrifice Qurban قربان

    We believe not any Messenger until he brings to us a sacrifice (3:183)
    See also 5:27, 46:28

Sacrificial offering Nusuk نسك See Ritual sacrifice

Safa Safa صفا

    Safa and Marva are among the waymarks of God (2:158)

Safety Salam سلام See Peace

Saiba Saibah سائبة

    God has not appointed cattle dedicated to idols, such as Bahira, Saiba (5:103)

Salih Salih صالح

Sent to Thamood 7:73, 11:61
Asked for what he threatened 7:77
A source of hope 11:62
He and his followers saved 11:66
He questioned 26:142

Salsabil Salsabil سلسبيل

Therein a fountain whose name is called Salsabil (76:18)

Salvation Furqan فرقان

When We gave to Moses the Book and the salvation
See also 2:185, 3:4, 8:29, 41, 21:48, 25:1

Samaritan Samiri سامري See Samiri

Same manner Shakila شاكلة

Every man works according to his own manner (17:84)

Samiri Samiri سامري

The Samaritan has misled them into error (20:85)
See also, 20:87, 95

Sanctury Bayt بيت See House

Satan Shaytan شيطان

Excites enmity and hatred 5:91
Resists His suggestion 7:200-201
Deceives 8:48
Reproaches own followers 14:22
Evil spirit, rejected accursed 3:36, 15:17, 34, 16:98
Has no authority over Believers 16:99-100
Suggests vanity 22:52-53
Is an enemy 35:6, 36:60

Satisfaction Mardat مرضاة See Good pleasure

Satisfaction Ridwan رضوان See Good pleasure

Saul Talut طالوت

> God has raised up Saul for you as king (2:247)
> See also, 2:249

Save Raqabah رقية See Neck

Save vt 'Asama عصم See Defend

Save vt Najja نجى See Deliver

Savour Sibghah صبغة See Baptism

Scales Mizan ميزان

> He whose scales are heavy – they are the prosperers (7:8)
> He whose scales are light - they have lost their souls (23:103)
> See also 6:152, 7:9, 85, 11:84, 85, 21:47, 23:102, 42:17, 55:7, 8, 9, 57:25, 101, 6, 8

Scales Mizan ميزان See Balance

Scatter Dhara'a ذرع

> It is He who scattered you in the earth (23:79)
> We have created for Gehenna many jinn and men (7:179)
> See also 6:136, 16:13, 42:11, 67:24

Scoop up with the hand Ightarafa إغترف

> He is of me, saving him who scoops up with his hand (2:249)

Screamer Taghiyah طاغية

> As for Thamood, they were destroyed by the Screamer (69:5)

Scroll Sijill سجل

On the day when We shall roll up heaven as a scroll is rolled for the writings (21:104)

Scum Ghutha غثاء

The cry seized them justly and We make them as scum (23:41)
See also 87:5

Sea Bahr بحر

Permitted to you is the game of the sea (5:96)
It is He who subjected to you the sea (16:14)
It is He who conveys you on the land and the Sea (10:22)
He knows what is in the land and the sea (6:59)
Not equal are the two seas (35:12)
See also 2:50, 164, 6:63, 97, 7:138, 163, 10:90, 14:32, 17:66, 67, 70, 18:60, 61, 63, 79, 109, 20:7, 22:65, 24:40, 25:53, 26:63, 27:61, 63, 30:41, 31:27, 31, 42:32, 44:24, 45:12, 52:6, 55:19, 24, 81:6, 82:3

Seal Khatam, Khitam ختم، ختام

Muhammad is not the father of any one of your men but the Messenger of God and the seal of the prophets (33:40)
Whose seal is musk so after that let the strivers (83:26)

Secret Ghayb غيب

Righteous women are therefore obedient, guarding the secret (4:34)
See also 2:3, 33, 3:44, 179, 5:94, 109, 116, 6:50, 59, 73, 7:188, 9:78, 94, 105, 10:20, 11:31, 49, 123, 12:52, 81, 102, 13:9, 16:77, 18, 38, 36:11, 39:46,49:18,50:33, 52:41, 53:35, 57:25,59:22,62:8,64:18,67:12,72:26, 81:24

Secret Khafiyah خافية

On that day you shall be exposed, not one secret of yours concealed (69:18)

Secretly Khufyah خفية

> Call on your Lord, humbly and secretly (7:55)
> See also 6:63

Security Amanah أمانة

> Then He sent down upon you, after grief, securing (3:154)
> See also 8:11

Security Mafazah مفازة

> God shall deliver those that were god fearing in their security (39:61)
> See also, 3:188

Seek Bagha بغى See Be insolent

Seek refuge Istaadha استعاذ

> Seek refuge in God (7:200)
> See also 16:98, 40:56, 41:36

Sect Shiah شيعة

> Pharaoh had exalted himself in the land and had divided its inhabitation's into sects (28:4)
> See also 6:65,15:10,19:69,28:15,30:32,34:54,37:83, 54:51

Selling Baye بيع See Trafficking

Send down vt Nazzala نزل

> God has sent the fairest discourse as a Book (39:23)
> It is He who sends down upon His servant signs (57:9)
> See also 2:23, 90, 97, 105, 176, 3:3, 93, 115, 4:47, 136, 140, 5:101, 115, 6:7, 37, 81, 111, 114, 7:33, 71, 196, 8:11, 9:64, 15:6, 9, 16:2, 44, 89, 102, 17:282, 93, 95, 106, 20:4,

80, 22:71, 24:43, 25:1, 25, 32 , 26:4, 192, 198, 30:24, 49, 31:34, 32:2, 36:5, 39:1, 23, 40:2, 13, 41:2, 42, 42:27, 28, 43:11, 31, 45:2, 46:2, 47:2, 20, 26, 50:9, 56:43, 80, 57:9, 67:9, 69:43, 76:23

Send forth Ba'atha بعث

We sent forth among every nation a Messenger (16:36)

We raised you up after you were dead (2:56)

Thy Lord will raise thee up to a laudable station (17:79)

See also 2:56, 129, 213, 246, 247, 259, 3:164, 4:35, 5:12, 31,6:2, 29, 36, 60, 65,7:14, 103, 167, 10:74, 75, 11:7 16:21, 36, 38, 84, 89, 17:5, 15, 59, 75, 79, 94, 98, 18:12, 19, 19:15, 35, 22:7, 23:16, 37, 82, 100, 25:41, 51, 25:41, 51, 26:87, 27:65, 28:59, 30:56, 31:28, 36:52, 37:16, 38:79, 40:34, 56:47, 58:6, 18,62:2, 64:7, 72:7, 83:4

Send vt Arsala أرسل

We have sent thee with the truth, good tidings to bear (2:119)

We sent Messengers before thee (13:38)

See also 2:151, 4:64, 79, 80, 5:70, 42, 7:59, 94, 133, 162, 9:33, 11:25 96, 12:19, 31, 109, 13:30, 38, 14:4, 5, 16:43, 63, 17:54, 77, 105, 19:17, 83, 20:134, 21:7, 25, 107, 22:52, 23:23, 32, 43, 45, 25:20, 48, 56, 26:53, 27:45, 28:47. 29'14. 40, 30:47, 51, 33:9, 45, 34:16, 28, 34, 44, 35:9, 24, 36:14, 37:72, 147, 40:23, 70, 78, 41:16, 42:48, 43:6, 23, 45, 46, 48:8, 28, 51:38, 41, 54:19, 31, 34, 57:25, 26, 61:9, 71:1, 73:15, 105:3

Sense of seeing Basar بصر See Eye

Sent Rih ريح See Wind

Sentinel Raqib رقيب See Observer

Servant Abd عبد

> God is never unjust unto His servants (3:182)
> He is aware of and sees His servants (17:30)
> God is gracious unto whomsoever He will of His servants (14:11)
> See also 2:23, 90, 178, 186, 207,221, 3:15, 20, 30, 79, 4:118, 172, 5:118, 6:18, 61, 88, 7:32, 128,194,8:41, 51, 9:104,10:107, 12:24,14:31, 15:40, 42, 49, 16:2,75, 17:1, 3, 5,17,53, 65, 96, 18:1, 65, 102, 19:2, 30, 61, 63, 93, 20:77,21:26, 105, 22:10, 23:109, 24:32,25:1,17, 58, 63, 26:52, 27:15, 19, 59, 28:82, 29:56, 62,30:48, 34:9, 13, 39, 35:28,31,32, 45, 36:46, 53, 40:15, 31, 44, 48, 85, 41:46, 42:19, 23, 25, 27,52, 43:15, 19, 59, 68, 44:18, 23, 50:8, 29, 53:10, 54:9,57:9, 66:10, 50:11, 71:27, 72:19, 76:6, 89:29, 96:10

Serve vt Abda عبد

> Thee only we serve (1:5)
> I am forbidden to serve those you call on (6:56)
> See also 2:83, 133, 172, 3:64, 5:76, 7:70. 9:31, 10:18, 28, 104, 11:2, 26, 62, 87, 109, 12:40, 13:36, 14:10, 35, 16:73, 114, 17:23, 18:16, 19:42, 44, 49, 21:66, 67, 98, 22:11, 71, 24:55, 25:17, 55, 26:70, 71, 75, 92, 17:43, 91, 28:63, 29:17, 34:40, 41, 43, 36:22, 60, 3722, 85, 95, 161, 39:3, 11, 14, 17, 64, 40:66, 41:14, 37, 43:26, 46:21, 51:56, 60:4, 98:5, 106:3, 109:2,3,5

Set forth by night Asra أسرى See Travel by night

Set free Harrar حرر

> They shall set free a slave (58:3)
> Let him set free a believing slave (4:92)
> See also 4:192, 5:89

Settle Aslaha أصلح See Make amends

Severe Fazz فظ See Harsh

Sexual desire Irbah اربة

    Such man as attend them, having sexual desire (24:31)

Share Khalaq خلاق

    Knowing well that whoso buys it shall have no share in the world to come (2:102)
    See also 2:200, 3:77, 9:69

Sharp Hadid حديد

    They flay you with sharp tongues (33:19)
    See also 50:22

Shechina Sakinah سكينة

    The Ark will come to you in it a Shechina from your Lord (2:248)
    See also 9:26, 40, 48:4, 18, 26

Shelter vt Awa أوى See Give refuge

Ship Fulk فلك

    When they embark in the ships, they call on God (29:65)
    He who conveys you on the land and the sea; and when you are in the ship (10:22)
    He subjected to you the ships to run upon the sea (14:32)
    God is He who has subjected to you the sea, that the ships may run on it (45:12)
    See also 2:164, 7:64, 10:73, 11:37, 38, 16:14, 17:66, 22:65, 23:22, 27, 28, 26:119, 30:46, 31:31, 35:12, 36:41, 37:140, 40:80, 43:12

Shoot vt Rama رمى See Throw

Shooting star Shihab شهاب See Avarice

Show Bayyana بين See Make clear, manifest

Shuaib Shuayb شعيب

    Sent to Midian 7:85, 11:84, 29:36
    Threaten to be ousted 7:88
    Questioned 11:87
    Advised his people 26:177

Sight 'Ayn عين See Eye

Sight Basar بصر See Eye

Signify vt Awha أوحى See Reveal

Signs Ayat آيات

    Demanded by those without knowledge, clear to those with Faith 2:118
    In the creation of the heavens and earth 2:164, 3:190
    Made clear, that men may consider 2:219-220
    Sign of authority to the prophet Samuel 2:248
    Denial of 3:11, 108
    Rejecters, deaf and dumb, in darkness 6:39
    In all things 6:95-99
    Wicked demand special Signs 6:124
    Rejecters make excuse 6:156-158
    Consequences of rejection 7:36-41, 146-147
    Rejecters wrong their own souls 7:177
    Rejecters get respite 7:182
    Rejecters lose guidance 6:186
    Day and night as Signs 17:12
    In nature and all creation 10:5-6, 30:20-27, 45:3-6
    Self evident Signs the Book 29:49-51
    Winds and ships 30:46, 42:32-35

Ships 31:31
The night, son and moon 36:37-40
The Ark through the Flood, and similar ships 36:41-44
In this life 39:59
Rejecters deluded 40:63
Rain and revived Earth 41:39-40
In the farthest regions of the earth, and in their own souls 41:53
Rejected or taken in jest 45:8-9
On earth, in your ownselves, and heaven 51:20-23
Creation of man from seed 56:57-59
Death 56:60-62
Seed in the ground 56:63-67
Water 56:68-70
Fire 56:71-73
Mocked 68:15
Camels, sky, mountains, earth 88:17-20
Forces of nature 89:1-5
No special signs (miracle) given 6:109, 10:20, 13:7, 17:59

Sijjin Sijjin سجين

The Book of the libertines is in Sijjin (83:7)
See also 83:8

Similitude Mathal مثل

God is not ashamed to strike a similitude even of a gnat (2:261)
God strikes similitudes for men (24:35)
See also 2:17, 171, 214, 261, 264, 265, 3:59, 117, 6:122, 7:176, 177, 10:24, 11:24, 13:17, 35, 14:18,24,25,26, 45, 16:60, 74, 75, 76, 112, 17:48, 89, 18:12, 45, 54, 22:73, 24:34, 35, 25:9, 33, 39, 29:41, 43, 30:27, 28, 58, 36:13,

78, 39:27, 29, 43:8, 17, 56, 57, 59, 47:3,15,48:29, 56:23, 57: 20, 59:15,16,21,62:5,66:10,11, 74:31

Sin Dhanb ذنب

> Sufficiently is He aware of His servants' sins (25:58)
> God seized them because of their sins (3:11)
> Remember God, and pray forgiveness for their sins (3:135)
> See also 3:16, 31, 147, 193, 5:18, 49, 6:6, 7:100, 8:52, 54, 9:102, 12:29, 97, 14:10, 17:17, 26:14, 28:78, 29:40, 33:71, 39:53, 40:3, 11, 21, 55, 46:31, 47:19, 48:2, 51:59, 55:39, 61:12, 67:11, 71:4, 81:9, 91:14

Sin Junah جناح See Fault

Sin Sayyi'ah سئية See Evil

Sin vt Ajrama أجرم

> Then We took vengeance upon those who sinned (30:47)
> You will not be questioned concerning our sins (35:25)
> See also 6:55, 123, 124, 147, 7:40, 84,133, 8:8, 9:66, 10:13, 50, 75, 82, 11:35, 52, 116, 12:110, 15:12, 58, 18:49, 53, 19:86, 20:74, 102, 25:22, 31, 26:99, 200, 27:69, 28:17, 78, 30:12, 47, 55, 32:12, 22, 34:32, 34:25, 32, 36:59, 37:34, 43:74, 44:22, 37, 45:31, 46:25, 51:32, 54:4,55:41,43,68:35,70:11,74:41,77:18, 46,83:29

Sinai Sayna, Sinin سيناء، سنين

> A tree issuing from the Mount Sinai that bears oil seasoning (23:20)
> For Sinin 95:2

Sincere Nasuh نصوح

> Believe, turn to God in sincere repentance (66:8)

Sing the praises of God Awwaba أوب

> O you mountains, echo God's praises with him, and you birds (34:10)

Sinker Kunnas خنس

> The runners, the sinkers (81:16)

Sirius Shira شعرى See Dog Star

Skin Julud جلود

> He has appointed for you of the skins of the cattle (16:80)
> Their eyes and their skins bear witness against them (41:20)
> See also 4:56, 22:20, 39:23, 41:21,22

Slander Buhtan بهتان

> This is a mighty calumny (24:16)
> See also 4:20, 112, 156, 33:58, 60:12

Slander Ifk إفك

> Those who came with the slander are a band of you (24:11)
> See also 24:12, 25:4, 29:17, 34:43, 37:86, 151, 46:11,28

Slanderer Hammaz, Humazah هماز، همزة

> Backbiter, going about slandering (68:11)
> Woe unto every backbiter slanderer (104:1)

Slave 'Abd عبد See Servant

Slave girl Amah أمة

> A believing slave girl is better than an idolatress (2:221)
> See also 24:32

Small faults lamam لمم See Lesser offences

Soft wind Rukha رخاء

> We subjected to him the wind that ran at his commandment safely (38:36)

Soften vt Alan ألان

> And we softened for him iron (34:10)

Sojourn Mustaqarr مستقر

> In the earth a sojourn shall be yours, and enjoyment for a time (2:36)
> See also 6:67, 98, 7:24 11:6, 25:24, 66, 76, 36:38, 75:12

Soloman Sulayman سليمان

> Did not disbelieve 2:102
> Gave judgment 21:78
> The wind at his command 21:81
> Of his forces 27:17
> Ants 27:18
> The Hoopoe 27:22-44
> A mere body 38:34

Son Ibn إبن

> Wealth and sons are the adornment of the present world (18:46)
> Neither has He made your adopted sons your sons in fact (33:4)
> The day when neither wealth nor sons shall profit (26:88)
> See also 2:49, 132, 133, 146, 246, 3:14, 61, 4:11, 23, 5:18, 27, 6:20, 100, 7:27, 141,150,9:24,30,11:42,45, 12:67, 81, 87, 14:6, 35, 16:72, 17:6, 40, 18:46, 20:94, 23:55, 24:31, 26:88, 133, 33:55, 37:149, 53, 40:25, 43:16, 52:39, 58:22, 68:14, 70:11, 71:12, 74:13, 80:36

For children of Israel, 2:40, 47, 83, 122, 211, 246, 3:49, 93,5:12,32,70,72,78,100,7:105,134, 137, 138, 10:90, 93, 17:2, 4, 101, 104, 20:47, 80, 94, 26:17, 22,59, 197, 27:76, 32:23,40:53, 43:59, 44:30, 45:16, 46:10, 61:6,14

Speak Haddatha حدث See Tell

Speak truth Sadaqa صدق

God has spoken the truth (3:95)

Assuredly God knows those who speak truly (29:3)

See also 2:23, 31, 94, 111, 177, 3:17, 93, 95, 152, 168, 183, 4:87, 122, 5:113, 119, 6:40, 115, 143, 146, 7:70, 106, 194, 9:43, 119, 10:38, 48, 92, 11:13, 32, 12:17, 26, 27, 26, 27, 51, 82, 15:7, 64, 17:80, 19:54, 21:9, 38, 24:6, 9, 26:31, 84, 154, 187, 27:27, 49, 64, 71, 28:49, 29:3, 49, 32:28, 33:8, 23, 24, 35, 34:29, 36:48, 52, 37:157, 39:32, 74, 40:28, 44:36, 45, 25, 46:4, 16, 22, 47:21, 48:27, 49:15, 17, 51:5, 52:34. 54:55, 56:87,59:8, 62:6, 67:25, 68:41

Speck on the date-stone Naqir نقير See Date stone

Spend vt Anfaqa أنفق See Expend

Sperm-drop Nutfah نطفة

He created man of a sperm-drop (16:4)

See also 18:37, 22:5, 23:13, 14, 35:11, 36:77, 40:67, 53:46, 75:37, 76:2, 80:19

Spider 'Ankabut عنكبوت

The frailest of the houses is the house of the spider (29:41)

See also 29:41

Spirit Ruh روح

The spirit is of the bidding of my Lord (17:85)

His word that He committed to Mary, and a spirit from him

See also 2:87, 253, 5:110, 15:29, 16:2, 102, 19:17, 21:19, 26:193, 32:9, 38:72, 40:15, 42:52, 58:22, 66:12, 70:4, 78:38, 97:4

Split vt Faraja فرج

When heaven shall be split (77:9)

Spliter Faliq فالق

It is God who splits the grain and the date-stone (6:95)
See also 6:96

Spouseless (woman) Ayama أيامى See Unmarried

Spread Basata بسط See Stretch out

Spy Tajassasa تجسس

Do not spy, neither back bite one another (49:12)

Squanderer Mubadhdhir مبذر

Squanderers are brothers of Satan (17:27)

Staling Asin أسن

Therein are rivers with water unstaling (47;15)

Star Najm نجم

It is He who has appointed for you the stars (6:97)
And by the stars they are guided (16:16)
And the stars and the trees bow themselves (55:6)
See also 7:54, 16:12, 22:18, 37:88, 52:49, 53:1, 55:6, 56:75, 77:8, 81:2, 86:3

Stature Taqwim تقويم

We indeed created man in the fairest stature, (95:4)

Status tamathil تماثيل

> What are these statues unto which your are cleaning (2:52)
> See also (17:13)

Step Darajah درجة See Rank

Step-daughters Rabaib ربائب

> Your step-daughters who are in your care (4:23)

Sticking (in the threat) Ghussah غصة See Choking

Sticky vt Lazib لازب See Clinging.

Stinginess Shuhh شح See Avarice

Stipulate vt, 'Ahida عهد See Make a convenant

Stone Hajar حجر

> Fear the Fire whose fuel is men and stones (2:24)
> Your hearts became hardened thereafter and are like stones (2:74)
> To loose upon them stones of clay (51:33)
> See also 2:60, 74, 7:160, 8:32, 11:82, 15:74, 17:50, 66:6, 105:4

Stone vt Rajama رجم

> If you give not over, we will stone you (36:18)
> We adorned the lower heaven with lamps, and made them things to stone Satans (67:5)
> See also 11:91, 18:20, 22, 19:46, 44:20, 26:116

Stoned Rajim رجيم See Accursed

Strange Fariy فري See Monstrous

Strength Azr ازر

By him confirm my strength (20:31)

Strength Ayd أيد See Might

Stress Ba's بأس See Might

Stretch out Basata بسط

> I will not stretch out my hand against thee (5:28)
> He outspreads and straightens His provision (42:12)
> He spreads them in heaven how He will (30:48)
> See also 2:245,5:11,28,64,6:93,13:14,16,17:29,30, 18:18, 28:82, 29:62, 30:37, 34:36, 39:52, 42:12, 60:2

Struggle Jahada جاهد

> Struggle in God's way with your possessions and yourselves (9:41)
> O Prophet struggle with the unbelievers and the hypocrites (66:9)
> God has preferred in rank those who struggle (4:85)
> See also 2:218, 3:142, 4:95, 5:35, 54,8:72, 74, 75, 9:16,19, 20,24,41, 44, 81, 86, 16:110, 22:78, 25:53, 29:6,8,69, 31:15, 49:15,60:1,61:11,66:9

Struggle vt Jahada جاهد

> Struggle in God's way with your possession and yourselves (9:41)
> O Prophet, struggle with the unbelievers and hypocrites (9:73)
> See also 2:218, 3:142, 5:35, 54, 8:72, 74, 75, 9:16, 19, 20, 44, 73, 81, 86, 88, 16:110, 22:7, 8, 15:52, 29:68, 69, 86, 31:15, 49:15, 61:11, 66:9

Study Allama علم See Teach

Stumps of trees Ajaz أعجاز

As if they were the stumps of fallen down palm trees (69:7)
See also 54:20

Subject vt Sakhkhara سخر

He subjected the sun and the moon each one running to a term stated (13:2)
Glory be to Him who has subjected this to us (43:13)
See also 2:164, 7:54, 14:32, 33, 16:12 14, 79, 21:79, 22:37, 65, 29:61, 31:20, 29, 35:13, 38:18, 36, 39:5, 43:13, 45:12, 13, 69:7

Sublime Aliy علي See High

Submission Silm سلم See Peace

Submissive Dhalul ذلول

It is He who made the earth submissive to you (67:15)
See also, 2:71, 16:69

Submit vt Aslama أسلم

Whosoever submits his will to God being a good doer (2:112)
Who is there that has a fairer religion than he who submits his will to God (4:126)
See also 2:128, 131, 132, 133, 136, 3:19, 20, 52, 64, 67, 80, 83, 84, 102, 4:125, 5:3, 44, 111, 6:14, 71, 125, 163, 7:126, 9:74, 10:72, 84, 90, 11:12, 101, 15:2, 15,81, 89, 102, 21:108, 22:34, 43:69, 46:15, 48:16, 49:14, 17, 51:36, 61:7, 66:5, 68:35, 72:14

Submit vt Ata'a أطاع See Obey

Substance Mal مال See Goods

Substitute vt Baddala بدل

Then the evildoers substituted a saying (2:59)
We may exchange the likes of you (56:61)
See also 2:181, 211, 4:56, 6:34, 115, 162, 10:15, 64, 14:28, 48, 16:101, 18:27, 24:55, 25:70, 27:11, 30:30, 33:23, 62, 34:16, 35:43, 40:26, 48:15, 23, 50:61, 70:41, 76, 28

Subverted (city) Mutafikah مؤتفكة

And the Subverted City He also over threw (53:53)
See also 9:70, 69:9

Successor Khalifah خليفة

And appoints you to be successors in the earth (27:62)
See also 2:30, 6:165, 7:69, 74, 10:14, 73, 35:39, 38:26

Succour Maun ماعون See Charity

Succour vt Ghatha غاث

There after there shall come a year wherein the people will be succoured (12:49)
See also 18:29

Suffice Kafa كفى

God suffices as a protector (4:45)
Thy Lord suffices as a guardian (17:65)
God suffices as a witness (48:28)
See also 2:137, 3:124, 4:6, 45, 50, 55, 70, 79, 81, 132, 166, 171, 10:29, 13:43, 15:95, 17:14, 17, 65, 96, 21:47, 25:31, 58, 29:51, 52, 33:3, 25, 39, 48, 41:52, 46:8, 48:28

Sufficient Ghaniy غني See Rich

Superfluity Nafilah نافلة

We gave him Isaac and Jacob in superfluity (21:72)
See also 17:78

Supporter Adud عضد See Helper

Sura Surah سورة

> Then bring a sura like it, and call your witnesses (2:23)
> Then bring you ten suras the like of it, forged (11:13)
> See also 9:64, 86, 124, 10:38, 24:1, 47:20

Sure Matin متين

> I respite them — assuredly My guile is sure (7:183)
>
> See also 51:58, 68:45

Surrender vt Aslama أسلم

Surround Haqa حاق See Encompass

Suwa Suwa سواع

> Do not leave your gods, and do not leave Wadd, nor Suwa (71:23)

Swarms Ababil أبابيل See Bird

Swear Halafa حلف

> They Swear to you by God, to please you (9:62)
> See also 4:62, 5:89, 9:42, 56, 74, 95, 96, 107, 58:14, 18

Sweet (water) Furat فرات

> He who let forth the two seas, this one sweet (25:53)
> See also 35:12, 77:27

Sweet Adhb عذب

> It is He who let forth the two seas, this one sweet (25:53)
> See also (35:12)

Swell vt Raba ربا See Increase

T

Tablet Lawh لوح

    We wrote for him on the Tablets on everything an admonition (7:145)

    See also 7:150, 154, 54:13, 85:22

Take notice Adhina أذن See Give leave

Take refuge 'Adha عاذ

    I take refuge with God (2:67)

    I take refuge in my Lord and your Lord from every man (40:27)

    See also 2:67, 11:47, 19:18, 23:97, 98, 40:27, 44:20, 72:6, 113:1, 114:1

    Trafficking is like usury (2:275)

    God has permitted trafficking and forbidden usury (2:275)

    Hasten to God's rememberance and leave trafficking aside (62:9)

    See also 2:254, 9:111, 14:31, 24:37

Take refuge Awa أوى

    I will take refuge in a mountain (11:43)

    See also 11:80, 18:10, 16, 63

Tall Basiq باسق

    Tall palm-trees with spathes compact (50:10)

Talut Talut طالوت See Saul

Tamarisk-bushes Athl أثل

    Two gardens bearing bitter produce and tamarisk-bushes (34:16)

Tasnim Tasnim تسنيم

    And whose mixture is Tasnim (83:27)

Taste Dhaqa ذاق

    Taste the chatisement of eternity (10:52)
    So it tasted the mischief of its action (65:9)
    Every soul shall taste of death ;you shall surely (3:185)
    See also 3:106, 181, 4:56, 5:95,6:30,148, 7:22, 39, 8:14, 35, 50, 9:35, 10:52, 16:95, 21:35, 22:22, 29:55,57, 32:14, 20, 34:42, 35:37, 37:31, 38, 38:8, 57, 39:24, 44:49, 56, 46:34, 51:14, 54:14, 54:37, 39, 48, 59:15, 64:5, 65:9, 78:30

Teach Allama علم

    He taught him such as He willed (2:251)
    We have not taught him poetry (36:69)
    He will teach him the Book (3:48)
    See also 2:31,32,102, 129,151, 282, 3:48, 79, 164, 4:113, 5:4, 110, 6:91, 12:6, 21, 37, 68, 101, 16:103, 18:66, 20:71, 21:80, 26:49, 27:16, 36:69, 44:14, 49:16, 53:5, 55:2, 4: 62:2, 96:4,5

Tell Haddatha حدث

    Upon that day she shall tell her tidings (99:4)
    See also 2:76, 93:11

Temple Bayt بيت See House

Temptation Fitnah فتنة See Trial

Term Ajal أجل

    It is He who created you of clay, then determines a term (6:2)

But God will never defer any soul when its turn comes (63:11)

See also 2:231, 232, 234, 235, 282, 4:77, 6:2, 60, 128, 7:34, 135, 185, 10:11, 49, 11:3, 104, 13:2, 38, 14:10, 44, 15:5, 16:61, 17:99, 20:129, 22:5, 33, 23:43,28:28,29,29:5, 53, 30:8, 31:29, 35:13, 45,39:5, 42, 40:67, 42:14, 46:3, 63:10,11, 65:2, 4, 71:4

Test vt Bala بلا See Try

Test vt Ibtla ابتلى

That God might try what was in your breasts (3:154)
See also 2:124, 249, 3:152, 4:6, 23:30, 33:11, 76:2, 89:15, 16

Thamood Thamood ثمود

Their Messenger 7:73, 9:70
They disbelieved in God 11:68
A she camel was given to them 17:59
They denied Messengers 26:141
Their dwelling places 29:38
A thunderbolt 41:13
They denied warnings 54:23
They denied the clatterer 69:4
They were destroyed by the Screamer 69:5
They hollowed the rocks in valley 89:9
They denied insolence

Thank vt Shakara شكر

Whosoever gives thanks gives thanks only for his own soul's good (27:40)
If you are thankful, surely I will increase you (14:7)
See also 2:52, 56, 158, 172, 185,243, 3:123, 144, 145, 4:147, 5:6, 89, 6:53, 63, 7:10, 17, 58, 144, 189, 8:26,

10:22, 60, 12:38, 14, 78, 114, 121, 17:19, 21:80, 22:36, 23:78, 27:40, 73, 28:73, 29:17, 30:46, 31:12, 14, 32:9, 34:15, 35:12, 36:35, 73, 39:7, 55, 40:61, 45:12, 46:15, 56:70, 67:23, 76:3, 9, 22

Thankful Shakur شكور See All-thankful

Thankless Kafur كفور See Ungrateful

The Kabah Kabah كعبة

God has appointed the Kabah, the Holy House (5:97)
See also 5:95

Thicket Aykah أيكة

The dwellers in the thicket were evildoers (15:78)
See also 26:176, 38:13, 50:14

Threaten Wa'ad واعد See Promise

Thornless Makhdud مخضود

Mid thornless lote-trees (56:28)

Throw Rama رمى

But God threw (8:17)
See also 4:112, 24:4, 6, 23, 77:32, 195:4

Thunderbolt Saiqah صاعقة

The thunderbolt took you while you were beholding (2:55)
See also 2:19, 4:153, 13,14, 41:13, 17, 51:44

Thunderclap Saiqah صاعقة See Thunderbolt

Time Sa'ah ساعة See Hour

Time Ummah أمة See Nation

Tissue Mudgah مضغة

Then we created of the tissue bones (23:14)
See also 22:5, 23:4

Tongue Lisan لسان

We have sent no Messenger save with the tongue of his people (14:4)

And stretch against you their hands and their tongues (60:2)

See also 3:78, 4:46, 5:78, 16:62, 103, 116, 19:50, 97,20:27, 24:15, 24, 26:13, 84, 195, 28:34, 30:22, 33:19, 44:58, 46:12, 48:11, 75:16, 90:9

Torah Tawrat توراة

He sent down the Torah and the Gospel (3:3)
See also 3:48, 50, 65, 93, 5:43, 44, 66, 68, 110, 7:157, 9:111, 48:29, 61:6, 62:5

Torment Adhab عذاب See Punishment

Torrent Midrar مدرار

He will loose heaven in torrents upon you (11:52)
See also 6:6, 71:11

Torture Adhab عذاب See Punishment

Torture vt Adhdhaba عذب See Chastise

Tottering Har هار See Weak

Towa Tuwa طوى

Thou art in the holy valley, Towa (20:12)
See also 79:16

Tower Buruj بروج

Death will overtake you, though you should be in raised up towers (4:78)

See also 15:16, 25:61, 85:1

Trace Athar أثر See Foot-step, Remnant

Track Athar أثر See Footstep

Track Hubuk حبك

> By heaven with all its tracks (51:7)

Trade Tijarah تجارة See Merchandise

Trading Tifarah تجارة See Commerce

Transgress I'tada اعتدى See Commit transgression

Transgress vt 'Ada عدا

> Transgress not the Sabbath (4:154)
> Who seeks after more than that, they are the transgressors (70:31)
> See also 2:173, 6:108, 145, 7:163, 10:90, 16:115, 23:7, 26:166

Transgression 'Udwan عدوان See Enmity

Travel by night Asra أسرى

> Glory be to Him who carried His servant by night (17:1)
> See also 11:81, 15:65, 20:77, 26:52, 44:23

Treaty Mithaq ميثاق See Compact

Trial Fitnah فتنة

> We have appointed it as a trial for the evildoers (37:63)
> We try you with evil and good for a testing (21:35)
> See also 2:102, 191, 193, 217, 3:7, 4:91, 5:41, 71, 6:23, 7:155, 8:25, 28, 38, 73, 9:47, 48, 49, 10:85, 17:60, 21:111, 22:11, 53, 24:63, 25,:20, 29:10, 33:14, 39:49, 51:14, 54:27, 60:5, 64:15, 74:31

Tribe Ashirah عشيرة See Clan

Tribes of the children of Israel Ashat أسباط

> We revealed to Abraham, Ismael, Isac, Jacob, and the Tribes (4:163)
> See also 2:136, 140, 3:84, 7:160

Tribute Jizyah جزية

> Until they pay the tribute out of hand and have been humbled (9:29)

Tribute Kharaj, Kharj خراج، خرج

> Yet the tribute of thy Lord is better (23:72)
> For Kharj 18:94, 23:72

Tribution Darra ضراء See Hardship

Trick Khana خان See Betray

Triumph Fawz فوز

> He will have mercy on him; that is the manifest triumph (6:16)
> The inhabitants of paradise – they are the triumphants (59:20)
> Whosoever is removed from the Fire and admitted to Paradise, shall win the triumph (3:185)
> See also 4:13, 73, 5:119, 6:16, 9:20, 72, 89, 100, 111, 10:64, 23:111, 24:52, 33:71, 37:60, 40:9, 44:57, 45:30, 48:5, 57:12, 59:20, 61:12, 64:9, 85:11

Troop Shirdhimah شرذمة

> Behold, these are a small troop (26:54)

Troops Jund جند See Host

Trouble Khabal خبال

Had they gone forth among you, they would only have increased you in trouble (9:47)
See also 3:118

True Nasuh نصوح See Sincere

Trust Amanah أمانة

Let him who is trusted deliver his trust (2:283)
See also 4:58, 8:27, 23:8, 33:72, 70:32

Trust vt Itamana إئتمن

Let him who is trusted deliver his trust (2:283)

Trust vt Tawakkala توكل

In God we have put our trust (7:89)
In God the Believers put all their trust (3:122)
See also 122,159, 160, 4:81, 5:11, 23, 7:89, 8:2, 49, 61, 9:51, 129, 10:84, 11:56, 88, 124, 12:67, 13:30, 14:11, 12, 16:42, 99, 25:58, 26:217, 27:79, 29:59, 33:3, 48, 39:38, 42:10, 36, 58:10, 60:4, 64:13, 65:3

Try vt Bala بلى

We tried them with good things and evil (7:168)
We will try you with some thing of fear (2:155)
See also 2:49, 155, 3:186, 5:48, 94, 6:165, 7:141, 163, 8:17, 10:30, 11:7, 14:6, 16:92, 21:35, 27:40, 37:106, 44:33, 47:4, 31, 67:2, 68:17, 86:9

Tubba Tubba تبع

Are they better, or the people of Tubba (44:37)
See also 50:14

Tumble vt Inhara إنهار

A crumbling back that has tumbled with him (9:109)

Turn away vt ‘Ada عدا See Transgress

U

Ultimate Uqba عقبى See End

Unbelievers Kuffar كفار

    Plot in vain 8:36
    Past forgiven, if they repent 8:38, 9:11
    Break covenants 8:56
    Will not frustrate the godly 8:60-61
    Protect each other 8:73
    Described 9:73-78, 14:3
    Will wish they had believed 15:2
    Will bear double burdens 16:25
    To be covered with shame 16:27
    Dispute vainly 18:56-57
    Their efforts wasted 18:102-106
    Their arrogance 19:73-82; 35:43
    Deeds like mirage 24:40
    As in depths of darkness 24:40
    Mutual recriminations at Judgment 34:31-33
    Self-glory and separatism 38:2-14
    Dispute about the Signs of God 40: 4-6
    Hate Truth 43:78
    Will turn back from fight 48:25-26
    Vain fancies 52-35-44
    Give them not friendship but kind and just dealing 60:1-9
    Rush madly 70:36-39

Unburdening Hittah حطة See Humility

Unchaste Baghiy بغى

    Nor was thy mother a woman unchaste (19:28)
    See also 19:20

Uncircumcised Ghulf غلف

> They say, Our hearts are uncircumcised (2:88)
> See also 4:155

Understand vt 'Aqala عقل

> There are signs for a people having understanding (2:164)
> They have hearts to understand with (22:46)
> See also 2:44,73, 76, 170, 171, 242, 3:65, 118, 5:58, 103, 6:32, 151, 7:169, 8:22, 10:16, 42, 100, 11:51, 12:2, 109, 13:4, 16:12,67,21:10, 67, 22:46, 23:80, 24:61, 25:44, 26:28, 28:60, 29:35, 43, 63, 30:24, 28, 36:62, 68, 37:138, 39:43, 40:67, 43:3, 45:5, 49:4, 57:17, 59:14, 67:10

Understand vt Faqiha فقه

> We have distinguished the signs for a people who understand (6:98)
> The hypocrites do not understand (63:7)
> See also 4:78, 6:25, 65, 7:169, 8:65, 9:81, 87, 127, 11:91, 17:44,46,18:57, 93, 20:28, 48:15, 59:13, 63:37

Unfair Diza ضيزى

> That were indeed an unjust division (53:22)

Ungrateful Kafur كفور

> Surely man is ungrateful (22:66)
> God loves not any ungrateful traitor (22:38)
> See also 11:9, 17:27, 67, 31:32, 35:36, 42:48, 43:15, 76:3,24, 80:17

Ungrateful Kanud كنود

> Surely man is ungrateful to his Lord (100:6)

Unjust Diza ضيزي See Unfair

Unmarried Ayama (pl. of ayyim) أيامى

Marry the spouseless among you (24:32)

Unseen Ghayb غيب See Secret

Untrue Batil باطل See Falsehood

Upper chamber Ghurfah غرفة

> Those who fear their Lord—for them await lofty chambers (39:20)
> See also 25:75, 29:58, 34:37

Urge Hadda حض

> He never urged the feeding of the needy (69:34)
> See also 107:3

Usury Riba ربا

> God has permitted trafficking, and forbidden usury 2:275
> See also 2:276, 278, 3:140, 4:161, 30:39

V

Vainglory 'Izzah عزة See Glory

Valour Batsh بطش See Assault

Vanity Batil باطل See Falsehood

Vehemently Gharq غرق See Violently

Veil Ghishwah, Ghita غطاء، غشاوة

> A seal on their hearts and on their hearing, and on their eyes is a covering (2:7)
> See also 45:23
> For Ghita 18:101, 50:22

Veil Jalabib جلابيب

> And the believing women that draw their veils (33:59)

Veil Kinn كن

> We lay veils upon their hearts lest they understand it (6:25)
> See also 17:46, 18:57, 41:5

Veils Akinnah أكنه

> We lay veils upon their hearts lest they understand it (6:25)
> See also 17:46, 18:57, 41:5

Verify Ahaqqa أحق

> But God was desiring to verify the truth (8:7)
> God blots out falsehood and verifies the truth (42:24)
> See also 8:8, 10:82

Very strong Dhu Mirrah ذو مرة

> Very strong; he stood poised (53:6)

Vestment Libas لباس See Garment

Viceroy Khalifah خليفة See Successor

Victory Fawz فوز See Triumph

Vie in patience Sabara صابر See Excel in patience

Vigour Irbah إربة See Sexual desire

Vile Khabith خبيث See Corrupt

Vine Inab عنب

> Would any of you wish to have a garden of palms and vines (2:266)
> See also 6:99, 13:4, 16:11, , 67, 17:91, 18:32, 23:19, 36,34, 78:32, 80:28

Violent Sarsar صرصار See Clamorous

Violently Gharq غرق

> By those that pluck out vehemently (79:1)

Vision Ru'ya رؤيا

> O my son relate not thy vision to thy brothers (12:5)
> See also 12:43, 100, 17:60, 37:105, 48:27

Visit (Mecca) vt Itamara إعتمر

> Whosoever makes the pilgrimage to the House (2:158)

Void Hawa هواء

> Their glances never returned on themselves, their hearts void (14:43)

Vow vt Nadhara نذر

> Whatever vow you vow, surly God knows it (2:270)
> Let them fulfill their vows and go about (22:29)
> See also 3:35, 19:26, 76:7

W

Wadd Wadd ود

    Do not leave Waddm nor Suwa (71:23)

Wage Ajr أجر

    Their wage awaits them with their Lord (2:62)
    O my people, I do not ask of you a wage for this (11:51)
    Surely thou shall have a wage unfailing (68:3)
    See also 2:112, 262, 274, 277, 3:57, 136, 171, 172, 178, 185, 190, 4:24, 25, 40, 67, 74, 95, 100, 114, 146, 152, 162, 173,5:5, 9, 6:90, 7:113, 170, 8:28, 9:22, 120, 10:72, 11:11, 29, 51, 115, 12:56, 57, 90, 104, 16;41, 96, 97, 17:9, 18:2, 30, 77, 25:57, 26:41, 109, 127, 145, 164, 180, 28:25, 54, 29:27, 58, 33:29, 31, 35, 44, 50, 34:47, 35:30, 36:11, 21, 38:86, 39:10, 35, 74, 41:8, 42:23, 40, 47:36, 48:10, 16, 29,48:3, 52:40, 57:7, 11, 18,19, 27, 60:10, 64:15, 65:5,6, 67:12, 68:46, 73:20, 84:25, 95:6

Walk with joy Harara هرر See Make joyful

Wander about vt Tafa طاف See Go round

Wander Dalla ضل See Go astray

Want Imlaq إملاق See Poverty

Ward off evil Ittaqa اتقى See Fear

Warning Dhikra ذكرى See Reminder

Wash Ghasala غسل

    O believers when you stand up to pray wash your faces (5:6)

Wasila Wasilah وسيلة

    Idols, such as Bahira, Saiba, Wasila, Hami (5:103)

Warning Dhikra, Tadhkirah ذكرى، تذكرة See Reminder

Waste Ada 'a أضاع

    God would never leave your faith to waste (2:143)
    I waste not the labour of any that labours among you (3:195)
    God leaves not to waste the wage of the believers (3:171)
    See also 7:170, 9:120, 11:115, 12:56, 90, 18:30, 19:59

Watch over Hafaza حافظ See Be watchful

Watch vt. Tahajjada تهجد See Keep vigil

Watcher Hafiz حفيظ See Guadian

Way Hubuk حبك See Track

Way mark Mash'ar مشعر

    Then remember God at the Holy Waymark (2;198)

Way mark Nusub نصب See Idol

Way Wasilah وسيلة See Mean

Way Wasilah وسيلة See Means

Weak Har هار

    Who founded his building upon the brink of a crumbling bank (9:109)

Weariness Lughub لغو See Fatigue

Well designed carpet Abqariy عبقري See Drugged

Well Trained Dhalul ذلول See Submissive

Well-informed Hafiy حفى See Guardian

Whistling Muka مكاء

> Their prayer of the House is nothing but a whistling (8:35)

Wholesome Hani هنى

> Eat and drink, with wholesome apetite
> See also 4:4, 69:24, 77:43

Wicked Bur بر See Corrupt

Wide eyed 'In عين

> We shall espouse them wide-eyed houris (44:54)
> See also 37:48, 52:20, 56:22

Wind Rih ريح

> God is He that looses the winds that stir up clouds (30:48)
> And to Solomon the wind strongly blowing (21:81)
> See also 2:164, 3:117, 7:57, 8:46, 10:22, 12:94, 14:18, 15:22, 17:69, 18:45, 22:31, 25:48, 27:63, 30:46, 51, 33:9, 34:12, 35:9, 38:36, 41:16, 42:33, 46:24, 51:41, 54:19, 69:6

Wine Khamr خمر

> Wine and arrow-shuffling idols and divining arrows are an abomination (5:90)
> See also 2:219, 5:91, 12:36, 41, 47:15

Wisdom Hikmah حكمة

> He gives the wisdom to whomsoever He will (2:269)
> Whoso is given the wisdom, has been given much good (2:269)

See also 2:129, 151, 131, 151, 3:48, 81, 164, 4:54, 113, 5:110, 16:125, 17:39, 31:12, 33:34, 30,20, 43:63, 54:5, 62:2

Wise Dhu Mirah ذو مرة See Very strong

Withering Aqim عقيم See Barren

Withhold Kaffa كف See Restrain

Witness Shahid شهيد

Call your witness, apart from God if you are truthful (2:23)
That you might be witness to the people (2:143)
See also 2:133, 143, 282, 3:98, 99, 140, 4:33, 41, 69, 72, 79, 135, 159, 166, 5:8, 44, 117, 6:19, 144, 150, 10:29, 46, 13:43, 16:84, 89, 17:96, 22:17, 78, 24:4, 6, 13, 28:75, 29:52, 33:55, 34:47, 35:69, 41:47, 53, 46:8, 48:28, 50:21, 37, 57:19, 58:6, 85:9, 100:7

Womb Arham أرحام

It is he who forms you in the womb as He will (3:6)
We establish in the wombs what we will (22:5)
See also 2:228, 4:1, 6:143, 144, 8:75, 13:8, 31:34, 33:6, 47:22, 60:3

Wonderful Ujab عجب See Marvellous

Wood Aykah أيكة See Thicket

Wool Ihn عهن

The mountain shall be as plucked like wool tufts (70:9)
See also 101:5

Wool tufts Ihn عهن See Wool

Word Kalimah كلمة

The likeness of a corrupt word is as a corrupt tree (14:26)
To Him good words go up (35:10)
No man can change His words (18:27)
See also 2:37, 124, 3:39, 45, 64, 4:46, 171, 5:13, 41, 6:34, 115, 7:137, 158, 8:7, 9:40, 74, 10, 19, 33, 64, 82, 96, 11:110, 119, 14:24, 26, 18:5, 278, 109, 20:129, 23:100, 31:27, 35:10, 37:171, 39:19, 71, 40:6, 41:45, 42:14, 21, 24, 43:28, 48:28, 49:26, 66:12

Work 'Amila عمل See Do

World Duniya دنيا

God gave them the reward of this world (3:148)
Good for those who do good in this world good (16:30)
See also 2:85, 86, 114, 130, 200, 201, 204, 212, 217, 230, 2:14, 22, 45, 56, 117, 145, 148, 152, 185, 4:74, 77, 94, 109, 134, 5:33, 41, 6:29, 32, 70, 130, 7:32, 51, 152, 156, 8:42, 67, 9:38, 55, 69, 74, 85, 10:7, 23, 24, 64, 70, 88, 98, 11:15, 60, 12:101, 13:26, 34, 14:327, 16:30, 41, 107, 122, 18:28, 45, 46, 104, 20:72, 131, 22:9, 11, 15, 23:33, 37, 24:14, 19, 23, 33, 28:42, 60, 61, 77, 79, 29:25, 27, 64, 30:7, 31:15, 33, 33:28, 57, 35:5, 37:6, 39:10, 26, 40:39, 43, 51, 41:12, 16, 31, 42:20, 36, 43:32, 35, 45:24, 35, 46:20, 47:36, 53:29, 57:20, 59:3, 67:5, 79:38, 87:16

Worlds Alamin عالمين See All beings

Worship vt. Abada عبد See Serve

Worth Ahl أهل

He is worthy to be feared (74:56)
See also 48:26, 74:56

Wrack Ghutha غثاء See Scum

Wrath Ba's بأس See Might

Wrath Ghadab غضب See Anger

Wretched Ba 'is بئيس

    Eat thereof, and feed the wretched poor (22:28)

Wrong Bagha بغى See Be insolent

Wrong vt Zalama ظلم

    God wronged them not (3:117)

    But they wronged themselves (11:101)

    See also 2:35, 51, 54, 57, 59, 92, 95, 124, 145, 150, 165, 193, 229, 231, 246, 254, 258, 270, 272, 279, 281, 3: 25, 57, 86,94,117,128, 135, 140,151,161,192, 4:10, 30, 40, 49, 75, 77, 97, 110, 124, 153, 160, 5:29, 39,6:21, 33,45, 47, 52, 58, 68, 98, 7: 9,19,23, 83, 181, 148, 160, 162, 165, 177, 8:25, 54, 60, 9:19,23,36,47, 70,109, 10:13, 39,44, 47,52, 54, 11:18, 31, 37, 44, 67, 83, 94, 101, 102, 113, 116, 12:23, 75, 79, 14:13, 22, 27, 42, 44, 45, 16:33, 85, 118, 17:33, 47, 59,71, 82, 99, 17:71, 18:29, 35, 50, 59, 87, 19:38, 60, 72, 21:2,11,14,29, 46, 47, 59, 64, 87, 97, 22:45, 48, 53, 71, 23:27, 28, 62, 24:50, 25:8, 27. 37, 26:10, 209, 227, 27:11, 44, 52, 85, 28:16, 21, 25, 29:14, 31,37, 40, 46, 49, 50, 30:29, 57, 31:11, 34:19, 31, 42, 35:32, 37, 40, 36:54, 37:63, 113, 37:22, 38:24, 39:24, 47, 51, 69, 40:52, 42:8, 21, 22, 40,44, 45, 43:39, 65, 76, 45:19, 22, 46:10, 12, 19, 49:11, 51:59, 52:47, 60:9, 61:7, 62:57, 65:1, 66:11, 68:29, 71:24, 28, 76:31

Y

Ya'uq Yauq يعوق

> Neither Nasr (71:23)

Yaghuth Yaguth يغوث

Yaguth, Ya'uq, يعوق

> Yaguth, Yauq, neither Nasr (71:23)

Yathrib Yathrib يثرب

> O People of Yathrib, there is no abiding here for you (33:13)

Z

Zachariah Zakariya زكريا

    Takes charge of Mary 3:37
    Find sustenance with her 3:37
    He called his Lord 3:38
    Was righteous 6:85
    His servant 19:2
    Was given good tidings of son 19:7
    His call for any heir 21:89

Zaid Zyad زيد

    When Zaid had accomplished what he would of her, then We gave her in marriage (33:37)

Zakat Zakat زكاة See Alms

Zakkoum Zaqqum زقوم

    You shall eat of a tree called Zakkoum (56:52)
    See also 37:62, 44:4

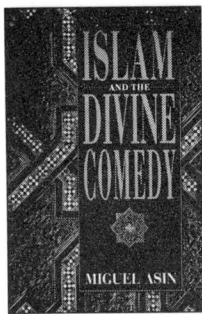

Goodword Books

- Tell Me About the Prophet Muhammad (HB)
- Tell Me About the Prophet Muhammad (PB)
- Tell Me About the Prophet Musa (HB)
- Tell Me About Hajj (HB)
- Tell Me About Hajj (PB)
- Tell Me About the Creation
- Honeybees that Build Perfect Combs
- The World of Our Little Friends, the Ants
- Life Begins: Quran Stories for Little Hearts (PB)
- The Ark of Nuh (HB)
- The Ark of Nuh (PB)
- The First Man (HB)
- The First Man (PB)
- The Two Brothers (HB)
- The Two Brothers (PB)
- The Brave Boy
- The Queen and the Bird
- Allah's Best Friend
- Tale of A Fish (PB)
- The Travels of the Prophet Ibrahim (PB)
- The Origin of Life (Colouring Book)
- The First Man on the Earth (Colouring Book)
- The Two Sons of Adam (Colouring Book)
- The Ark of Nuh and the Animals (Colouring Book)
- The Brave Boy (Colouring Book)
- Allah's Best Friend (Colouring Book)
- The Travels of the Prophet Ibrahim (Colouring Book)
- The Ark of Nuh and the Great Flood (Sticker Book)
- The Story of the Prophet Nuh (HB)
- The Story of the Prophet Nuh (PB)
- The Blessings of Ramadan (PB)
- The Story of Prophet Yusuf (PB)
- The Holy Quran (PB)
- The Holy Quran (HB)
- Islam Rediscovered
- A Dictionary of Muslim Names
- The Most Beautiful Names of Allah (HB)
- The Most Beautiful Names of Allah (PB)
- The Pilgrimage to Makkah
- Arabic-English Dictionary for Advanced Learners
- The Spread of Islam in the World
- A Handbook of Muslim Belief
- The Muslims in Spain
- The Moriscos of Spain
- The Story of Islamic Spain (PB)
- Spanish Islam (A History of the Muslims in Spain)
- A Simple Guide to Muslim Prayer
- A Simple Guide to Islam
- A Simple Guide to Islam's Contribution to Science
- Islamic Medicine
- Islam and the Divine Comedy
- The Travels of Ibn Jubayr
- The Travels of Ibn Battuta
- Humayun Nama
- The Arabs in History
- Decisive Moments in the History of Islam
- My Discovery of Islam
- Islam At the Crossroads
- The Spread of Islam in France
- The Islamic Art and Architecture
- The Islamic Art of Persia
- The Hadith for Beginners
- How Greek Science Passed to Arabs
- Islamic Thought and its Place in History
- Muhammad: The Hero As Prophet
- A History of Arabian Music
- A History of Arabic Literature
- The Qur'an for Astronomy
- Islamic Economics
- The Quran
- Selections from the Noble Reading
- The Koran
- Heart of the Koran
- Muhammad: A Mercy to All the Nations
- The Sayings of Muhammad
- The Beautiful Commands of Allah
- Allah is Known Through Reason
- The Miracle in the Ant
- The Miracle in the Immune System
- The Miracle in the Spider
- Eternity Has Already Begun
- Timelessness and the Reality of Fate
- Ever Thought About the Truth?
- Crude Understanding of Disbelief
- Quick Grasp of Faith
- Death Resurrection Hell
- The Basic Concepts in the Quran
- The Moral Values of the Quran
- The Beautiful Promises of Allah
- The Muslim Prayer Encyclopaedia
- After Death, Life!
- Living Islam: Treading the Path of Ideal
- A Basic Dictionary of Islam
- The Muslim Marriage Guide
- GCSE Islam–The Do-It-Yourself Guide
- A Treasury of the Quran
- The Quran for All Humanity
- The Quran: An Abiding Wonder
- The Call of the Qur'an
- Muhammad: A Prophet for All Humanity
- Words of the Prophet Muhammad
- An Islamic Treasury of Virtues
- Islam and Peace
- Introducing Islam
- The Moral Vision
- Principles of Islam
- Indian Muslims
- God Arises
- Islam: The Voice of Human Nature
- Islam: Creator of the Modern Age
- Woman Between Islam and Western Society
- Woman in Islamic Shari'ah
- Islam As It Is
- Religion and Science
- Tabligh Movement
- The Soul of the Quran
- Presenting the Quran
- The Wonderful Universe of Allah
- The Life of the Prophet Muhammad
- History of the Prophet Muhammad
- A-Z Steps to Leadership
- The Essential Arabic
- One Religion
- The Way to Find God
- The Teachings of Islam
- The Good Life
- The Garden of Paradise
- The Fire of Hell
- Islam and the Modern Man
- Uniform Civil Code
- Man Know Thyself
- Muhammad: The Ideal Character
- Polygamy and Islam
- Hijab in Islam
- Concerning Divorce
- Search for Truth
- The Concept of God
- The Creation Plan of God
- The Man Islam Builds
- Non-Violence and Islam
- Islamic Fundamentalism
- The Shariah and Its Application
- Spirituality in Islam
- Islamic Activism
- Islam Stands the Test of History
- The Revolutionary Role of Islam
- Islam in History
- Conversion: An Intellectual Transformation
- A Case of Discovery
- Manifesto of Peace